MIAN DIDO: THE ROBIN HOOD OF JAMMU

Translated from Dogri to English

DR. ABHAI SINGH BHADWAL

ISBN 979-8-88935-905-0

Dedicated to my friends and family
who have supported me throughout my life and
my nephew whose laughter cheers up my world,
may this book encourage you to dream fearlessly in life.

Introduction
Kingdom of Jammu

In 1703, King Dhruv Dev ascended to the throne. He had four sons—Ranjit Dev, Dhansar Dev, Surat Singh, and Baldev Singh. After the death of Dhruv Dev in 1735, his eldest son, Ranjit Dev succeeded him.

Ranjit Dev was intelligent, brave, and a glorious king. The kingdom of Jammu prospered in his reign. Due to the innumerable vandals and dacoits, Punjab's plains had become a place of terror. For this reason, traders from Kabul and Kashmir travelled to Delhi via Jammu. This route went directly from Jammu to Basholi, Haripur, and Nurpur, towards Nadaun, Vilaspur, and then Nahan. Although longer, this route was free from the risks of the plains.

Thus, Jammu became a trading hub. Traders from other countries visited Jammu for the barter of goods. Here, warehouses were always full of goods. Due to such heavy trade frequency, Ranjit Dev treated the traders quite well.

He had two sons: the elder one was Brajraj Singh and the younger one, Dalel Singh. The elder son was an alcoholic and drug addict; hence, Ranjit Dev wanted his younger son to succeed him. This caused a rift between the elder son and the father.

Both called the Sikhs for their help on this matter. Jhanda Singh Bhangi took the side of the king, and Mahan Singh stood in favour of Brajraj Dev; and both exchanged their turbans and became brothers by religion. After some months, both Sikhs returned to their respective places, and Ranjit Dev kept his throne.

In 1781, Ranjit Dev passed away, and his elder son, Brajraj Dev, came to power and thought of putting his younger brother, Dalel Singh, to death. Surat Singh's son Zoravar Singh, who was a well-built young man, was called for this assignment but refused.

Then Brajraj Dev went to Surat Singh's elder son, Mian Mota. He agreed to do this for the king.

Dalel Singh, accompanied by his elder son, Bhagwant Singh Sasu, had gone on a pilgrimage to Trikuta Devi. Near the Charan Paduka village, they were attacked by Mian Mota. They both fought bravely but, in the end, lost their lives. Dalel Singh's younger son, Jeet Singh, tried to escape but was caught and placed under house arrest.

Mian Mota was given the rank of *wazir* (minister) in the court. In 1787, Sikhs again tried to invade Jammu. Brajraj Dev fought hard, but in the end, was killed. His son, Sampoorn Dev, who was just one year old at that time, was placed on the throne. In 1788, he died with his mother.

It was at that time when Mian Mota gave the throne to Dalel Singh's imprisoned son, Jeet Singh. But he proved to be a stupid king. He was under house arrest for so long that he showed no qualities typical of a king. But Mian Mota was a *wazir,* so he did whatever he liked. This caused the kingdom of Jammu to lose power day by day.

However, Jeet Singh's wife, who was the daughter of the king of Bandral, was very intelligent. She wanted to fire Mian Mota, but at that moment, Ranjit Singh attacked Jammu and became the new king of Jammu.

Surat Singh's grandson, Kishor Singh, migrated to Lahore and started serving there. His sons, Gulab Singh, Dhian Singh, and Suchet Singh became renowned ministers in the court of King Ranjit Singh. Gulab Singh reigned as the king of Jammu when the Britishers ascended.

Mian Dido

Mian Dido was a brave patriot who helped the poor, was kind towards them, and punished the cruel who did any harm to them. He was related to the royal family of Jammu.

When Ranjit Singh thought of annexing the Duggar land, Dido learned of his plan and found it unacceptable. He wanted his region to be independent as always. Dido gathered all the Dogras and threatened Mian Mota, who had betrayed the region and befriended Ranjit Singh.

In 1810, there was a huge clamour on the issue and forces were deployed from Lahore. Devan Singh from Reasi and many more were imprisoned. It was at this moment that two groups in Jammu were formed. On one side were Mian Mota and his companions, while on the other side were Mian Dido, Bhupdev, Jeet Singh's wife, and a few patriots.

Mian Mota was assassinated. Mian Dido took an oath that he would never let the Sikhs take hold of his region again.

Wherever he found a Sikh soldier, he put him to death. For a long time, the Sikhs in Jammu had a tough time and chaos prevailed there. The stories of Mian Dido's bravery and valour are still on the lips of the Dogras.

First Group

Characters in the Play

1. Maharaja Ranjit Singh: King of Punjab
2. Jeet Singh: King of Jammu
3. Mota Singh: Jeet Singh's *wazir* (minister).
4. Bishna, Badhana and Zoravar Singh: *Wazirs* of Jammu
5. Jagat Singh Kalal: *Subedar* (subordinate) of Ranjit Singh
6. Gulab Singh: Chief of the Army of Ranjit Singh

Second Group

1. Mian Dido: Patriot of Jammu and opponent of Ranjit Singh
2. Devan Singh: Landlord of Reasi
3. Bhupdev: Son of Devan Singh
4. Mian Hazari: Father of Mian Dido
5. Mian Channo Shripat and Dharam Singh Raipuria: Well-wishers of Dido
6. Triddu and Satru: Two murderers

Commoners

1. Baba Mihan Singh and Baba Mulkhraj: Enemies of Gulab Singh in the Court of Ranjit Singh
2. Narayan Singh, Mahna Singh, Gahna Singh: Soldiers of the Sikh army
3. Dainju, Thainnu, and Beli: Common people of Duggar who didn't belong to any side
4. *Kotwal* (policeman), *ardali* (one who conveys king's messages), *maali* (gardener), *sadhu* (saint), Bhat, Sarban, and *chabuk Savar* (whip-rider)

Women

1. Jeet Singh's wife (queen)
2. Thakurian: Dido's wife
3. Mangli: Dido's Mother's maid
4. Santi: Queen's maid
5. Pratapi: Housewife

Part I

Scene - 1

On an evening, Dido is seen with his *Thakurian* with a hawk in his hand in the mountains of Goddess Trikuta.

Dido: [To the hawk] Well done! Today, after a long time, you flew so high. I am very content! You are a sign of a superior soul.

Thakurian: Great King! You are superior to humans, and he is superior to birds. As you can't tolerate being subordinated by others, this bird too can't be imprisoned in a cage.

Dido: Hey, listen, dear. This world is a place for those who act and not for the parasites and idle ones. Here, nobody values them. The world is abuzz with activities from day to night. Learn from the mountains all around, the endless seas, the gushing waterfalls—each creature in this world constantly working from dusk to dawn. Learn from them and achieve all your dreams.

Thakurian: You are truly a *yogi*, and like other *Yogis*, you love being stoic. You are courageous. I believe that your courage will certainly succeed.

Dido: Dear wife, your wish is so pure; why will I doubt my success?

[People hailing from far away] *Jai Trikuta Maa! Jai*

Trikuta Maa!

Thakurian: What's this hailing?

Dido: The devotees are here after visiting the Goddess.

[Looking towards the devotees] Yes, brother.

What's the matter?

Man: Great King, Goddess Trikuta has shown a miracle.

Dido: Good! How?

Thakurian: Oh, brother, tell us what happened!

Man: Great King, the Goddess has given sight to a person who was blind from birth.

Thakurian: To a person blind from birth?

Man: Yes, *Mataji* (Mother)! To a person blind by birth.

Thakurian: *Jai Trikuta Maa!* Where is that man?

Man: *Mataji,* look behind. A large gathering is coming.

[A group of people are hailing and approaching the place. Along with them is a man seated inside a palanquin. The man's wife is running after him.]

Dido: Dear wife, see, the procession is coming along with that man.

Thakurian: Oh ho! Poor hapless man is so happy after getting eyes.

Dido: Wow! He will do more sin in the future.

Thakurian: Brother! Wait. I am coming to take a look at you.

[The men stop]

Dido: [To that man] Good man! Since when have you been blind?

Man: I am blind from birth.

Woman: Yes! He was blind from birth!

Thakurian: Who are you?

Woman: I am his wife.

Thakurian: How do you know that he was blind from birth?

Were you his mother or midwife at the time of his birth?

Dido: Where is his home?

Woman: Chenani.

Thakurian: Look, good man, Goddess Trikuta has blessed you. Cherish this favour forever!

Dido: How did you go to visit Goddess Trikuta? Did you just coincidentally happen to visit her, or did you go to pray for the sight?

Man: Great King, I came here for the sight only. The Goddess appeared in my dreams many times and said, "Come over here; I will mitigate your sufferings."

Woman: He is telling the truth. I have seen Goddess Trikuta calling him many times.

Dido: Oh! And you are lame too?

Man: Yes! As God wills.

Dido: How did you become lame?

Man: I fell from a tree.

Woman: Yes, he had fallen from a berry (Indian plum) tree.

Dido: Oh? Since when are you blind?

Man: Well, I am blind from birth.

Dido: Despite being blind, did you used to climb trees?

You seem to have been very naughty since childhood.

Man: Yes, I climbed a tree once, a very long time ago.

Woman: He is speaking the truth. He has climbed once.

Dido: Are you fond of eating berries?

Man: Sir, my wife forced me to climb the tree; I had no choice.

Dido: You are very clever. Show me your eyes.

[The man shows him his eyes.]

Dido: Just blink them. Now shut them, then blink again! I think you are still not able to see clearly.

Man: No, sir! I can. It is afternoon.

Dido: Really? Then tell me the colour of my *sutthan.*

Man: Sir, it's brown.

Dido: You are right. Now tell me, what is the colour of my *angarakha*?

Man: It is black – much like the colour of griddle soot.

Thakurian: How do you know that griddle's soot is black?

Dido: You must not have seen the griddle yet.

Thakurian: Have you seen *sutthan* and *angarkhas* before?

Woman: Not before today.

Dido: Okay, then tell me, what is my name?

Man: Great King, how would I know?

Dido: [Pointing towards Thakurian] Who is she?

Man: Forgive me, but how would I know?

Woman: He doesn't know anyone's name.

Dido: What is your name?

Man: My name is Sarban.

Dido: Sarban, I think you are lying. If you have been blind since birth, then how can you identify colours?

Sarban: I was born blind.

Dido: Sarban, Goddess Trikuta has really done a miracle by giving vision to a blind man. Now, if by my wisdom I correct your limping, will you accept my wisdom?

Sarban: I will be indebted to you for life and bless you.

Dido: Is there any *chabuk savar* (whip-rider) in the court?

One Man: Yes, too many.

Dido: Then go and bring a whip-rider.

[The man sends a boy with this message.]

Dido: Put this stone here **[A stone is pushed forward]** Look, Sarban! Jump over this stone and run back home.

Sarban: Shri Ram! Shri Ram! Great King, I can't even stand, let alone run.

Dido: If you will not jump, you will be hit by the whip.

[The whip-rider arrives with a horse.]

Sarban: Great King, are you joking with me?

Dido: I am not joking; I am telling the truth. If you will not jump over the stone, you will be hit by the whip.

Whip-rider: What is the order for me?

Dido: You must stand here until he jumps over this stone and runs away.

Whip-rider: As you order, Great King!

Dido: Sarban, get ready.

Sarban: Great King, I can't even stand. Why inflict pain on a hapless poor man?

Dido: Sarban, you must stand on your legs.

Whip-rider: Sarban, take off your *kurta.*

[Sarban takes off his kurta hesitantly and lamely approaches the stone.]

Dido: Sarban, jump over and run away.

[The king asks the whip-rider to hit him harder. The whip-rider hits harder. Sarban jumps over and runs like the wind. People run behind him. Thakurian can't stop laughing.]

Thakurian: See how he ran. Oh God! This world is full of fraudsters. My stomach is aching from laughing so hard.

Dido: [To the woman] Why did you create such a ruse?

Thakurian: You were saying that his legs were broken from falling off the berry tree.

Women: What to do? I made up this drama to fill my stomach.

Dido: Now leave. But if you do this again, I will kill you.

[CURTAINS]

Scene - 2

Wazir's House

[Mian Mota appears to be praying.]

Mota: [After the worship] I don't know why my parents named me 'Mota'. I'm thin and not stupid. I'm a good young man and have won so many battles. If Dalel Singh had been alive today, he would have got the throne. Then who would ask me? He had his ill fortune to visit Trikuta Maa. It's my good luck because he was unaware and alone. My plan succeeded; I owed Brajraj Dev by killing him along with his son. To be a *wazir* became my right. This all happened because of my sharp intelligence and not because of my stupidity. Brajraj only drank day and night, and that is why I became the king as well as the *wazir*. Then why is my name Mota? I think my parents were the stupid ones. They didn't know my capabilities. They gave me this name randomly. Yes, my luck is bad that's why they gave me that name. Now, Jeet Singh is the king. He is useless. But I will be the one to eternally rule here.

[Badhana and Bishanaa arrive]

Badhana: *Wazir* is just like a monk. No matter what happens to him, he doesn't understand.

Bishanaa: His aloof manner has spoiled everything. The scoundrels are becoming more daring.

Mota: Mian Bishanaa, those who follow this path will die on their own. Why are you worried?

Bishanaa: Listen, *wazir*! You held the kingdom for three generations and now you have become so bad that wastrels say anything about you that comes to their mind.

Mota: Then, what should I do?

Bishanaa: Stick to your words. To be righteous, you need not harm anyone, but you have to maintain fear of your authority.

Bandhana: *Wazir* says that God once reprimanded the snake for stinging people for no reason. The snake then pleaded with God, saying if he quit stinging, then people would make it difficult for him to live. God said, in that case, you don't quit your hissing. The point is, dear *wazir*, you surpassed that snake and quit your hissing too.

Mota: You are my hissing snakes! If I must suffer while you are by my side, what else can I do?

Bishanaa: Then you listen to what we say.

Mota: Tell me, what do you say?

Bishanaa: Press charges of sedition against Dido, Bhup, and their young accomplices. Seize the fiefdom of everyone. When it comes to the announcement, no one will be by their side. But we still need to do something, just to be sure.

Badhana: Now they are spreading rumours among people that you want to sell the kingdom to Maharaja Ranjit Singh.

Mota: I heard everything but said nothing. What will the world say?

Bishanaa: The world? Whoever utters a few words, people follow them. When their faults are pointed out, everyone will come to know.

Badhana: Dear *wazir*, the nature of the world is like the fickle of mercury. The way mercury rises and falls in summers and winters, similarly, the world changes in response to preaching and teaching. The world abruptly changes at every single moment.

Mota: Well, then what should I do with the queen?

She is furious.

Bishanaa: Wow! A woman's wisdom is always in her heel. You should lure her and she will come like a fly, come to honey; even though later she may regret it.

Mota: You want to say that by alluring her she will give up her stubbornness? Women's stubbornness is infamous in the world.

Bishanaa: Wazir, if it is infamous, so be it. But temptation is an important weapon in politics – it turns stone into wax and iron into water.

Mota: Then hand over the property to the queen.

Bishanaa: Yes, of course.

Mota: Can you convince the queen? **Bishanaa:** Dear *wazir*, you must try yourself. **Mota:** She won't even talk to me.

Bishanaa: Why won't she? What do you even know about politics?

Mota: Okay, you go. I will follow you.

Bishanaa: Okay. That's great.

[He leaves.]

[CURTAINS]

Scene - 3

[Women's Room]

[The Queen is sitting on the bed]

Maid: Your Highness, Mian Bishanaa wants to meet you.

Queen: Well, Santi, send him in.

[Santi goes to bring Bishanaa in]

Bishanaa: [Touching the feet] Your Highness.

Queen: Live long, Brave Bishanaa. What made you come here today?

Bishanaa: Your Highness, I went out.

Queen: Well, what news have you brought? **Bishanaa:** Your Highness, the *wazir* is coming to meet you.

Queen: Then today the sun will rise from the west.

But what is the need for the *wazir* to meet us? He is the king and can do as he pleases.

Bishanaa: Your Highness, the *wazir* always adheres to your orders. Whatever he does, he does for your welfare.

Queen: Well, the world will see everything.

Bishanaa: Yes, Your Highness. Please listen to the *wazir* first. Do not live in an illusion.

Santi: Your Highness, the *wazir* is here.

Queen: Call him.

[Santi goes and the *wazir* comes]

Mota: *Jai Raghunathji!* (Hail God), are you fine, Your Highness?

Queen: Yes, I'm fine *Wazir*. How come you're here?

Mota: Your Highness, the state is facing a rough time. It's difficult to distinguish who is ours and who is not. Whoever we shake hands of friendship with, ends up cheating.

Queen: Then what to do?

Mota: In such difficult times, only the women of the high clans can protect the empire with their intelligence and courage. So now our only hope is you.

Queen: Who needs my intelligence?

Mota: Raghunath, Raghunath. (Hail God). Your Highness, if we do not feel the need of your intelligence, then who would call us intelligent?

See, King Jeet Singh is not among the smartest people. Seeing all this, the rascals have become more active.

Their desire is to evict Jeet Singh from the seat and murder him. Would you like that?

Queen: You yourself are intelligent. I come from a different world anyway.

Mota: God bless you. Then you help us find a solution.

Queen: I will, Wazir. What would you suggest?

Mota: We have heard that the governing board is giving you different temptations; you are getting an axe to hurt your feet.

Queen: Someone has tried to provoke you by lying to you? Yes, but I'm sad that my kingdom is being sold for peanuts because of the greedy fraudsters around.

Mota: Enough. I understood that these insurgents have filled your ears well. Your Highness, how will the state be sold for peanuts?

As long as I'm alive, nothing can ruin the state. This governing board will surely get the fruits of their actions.

Queen: You think I am a fool who doesn't know anything about the king's profit and loss. I know well that the king is useless. He doesn't know the difference between friends and foes. Why should I not be sad?

Mota: What else are kings like? He is doing well.

Queen: Is this how a king should be? The people are not receiving justice. In the palace, he lives like an outsider. He doesn't even know anything about politics. You have destroyed his intelligence.

Mota: Your Highness, kings are like that. Brajraj Dev and all of the Devs were also like this. Jeet Singh's tenure will also pass like others. The state always runs on the shoulder of the *wazir*.

Even people say that, irrespective of how the king might be, if the minister is foolish then the state will crumble. But if the minister is sensible then even an owl can rule the state well.

I have been managing the state for three generations. This is a challenging period, and hence now it's time to enthrone you as the queen of the state.

Queen: I agree that you favour us a lot, but how long will you do all this? I don't possess enough strength to keep accepting someone's favour. What sort of person always depends on others their whole life? The wife of this kind of husband has no worth.

Mota: - Your Highness, you are speaking the truth. But this is what God wills. No one will leave their comfort for hardships. Neither does anyone want to leave the palace and live in a hut. If God has written discomfort and poverty in our destiny, can we do anything about it?

Your Highness, Jeet Singh is good or bad, but our fate is associated with him, not with anyone else.

Queen: I will handle the state affairs myself.

Mota: Oh, my God! You never say this in front of me. Should we send the bangle-wearing queen of the palace to sit in the court and get insulted from all over the world? Our respect will be lost. Are we dead? Who gives their honour into the hands of women?

Queen: Have women never ruled before?

Mota: Yes, women have ruled, but when they had no recourse. We are still alive; what is the need for women to take over the state?

Queen: If the man is a fool, and if the house is set on fire, will the woman keep watching the scene silently? Stand without doing anything? Who will be suffering more than me for the kingdom?

Mota: Your Highness, it is impossible. Where will our honour be left? All of us will be called women's servants and slaves. Women are soft in nature anyway –anyone comes and talks, flatters them, and gets his work done. A hard knot needs a strong set of teeth to undo it.

Queen: Why would you become a woman's servant? Be Ranjeet Singh's servant.

Bishanaa: Your Highness, listen with patience. The *wazir* is right. Dear *Wazir*, you give the estate to the queen. She will rule.

Mota: I'm ready to write today and ready to hand over such a beautiful area of Jaganaur to her.

Bishanaa: Wow! That's great.

Queen: Now shall I leave the state and take estate?

Mota: Does the state belong to someone else?

Queen: Do you want to evict me?

Mota: No, Your Highness! You will be the first consulted on State affairs. Bishanaa, write the order.

[Bishanaa writes]

[CURTAINS]

Scene 4

[Wazir's House]

[Mian Mota is in deep thought. Wazirani approaches him.]

Wazirani: Dear Husband, you've committed a serious mistake by installing Jeet Singh as the monarch. You yourself have laid thorns under your feet. You seemed to be intelligent and well-versed in politics; then why did you make this mistake? Was Ranjeet Dev not your brother? What happened if he was elder? He also wanted to hand over the kingdom to his younger son. Then how do you say that the elder son has the right to the throne? This is not a policy but an illusion of your mind. State thrones always reserve the authority to bestow honour on the deserving. You have entrusted the throne to Jeet Singh and you yourself have put the rope around your neck. When I go to the palace, my heart burns red-hot coals. I can't bear the tantrums of his wife.

[Mota looks at her angrily and ignores the matter]

Wazirani: Where is your attention? What are you thinking so deeply? Why are you not answering me?

[Mota rubs his eyes again]

Wazirani: I am saying, don't push away Goddess Lakshmi from the house. Don't you see Jeet Singh's crown studded with diamonds? Why aren't your eyes closed by the dazzle of his crown? Why wouldn't you dare to wear this crown on your head? If your hands don't reach there, join my hands too, and let's dignify our dignity.

Mota: Dear, why are you talking that way? Being my wife, how could you talk about temptations? Jeet Singh is my nephew. *Raghunath, Raghunath!* I get leprosy if such a thing even crosses my mind. I had a dream in the morning; I was engrossed in that thought.

Wazirani: What kind of a dream? Tell me! I also had a dream this morning; I will also tell you.

Mota: In the dream, it felt like someone broke my stamp. Who broke it is not known. Then it felt like Mian Dido broke my stamp. Then my stamp and my bag went into the hands of Kishor Singh. God bless everyone. I don't understand the meaning of this dream.

Wazirani: Even after being so smart, you couldn't understand it? God has indicated that you should leave the post of *wazir* and become the king. You are the eldest and wise. You know all the secrets of governance. Jeet Singh is not suitable for the kingdom. Kishor Singh will become your *wazir*.

Mota: *Raghunath! Raghunath!* This is not the meaning of my dreams. This is the improper thinking of your heart. Now you tell me what you dreamed.

Wazirani: Dear, I saw you sitting on the throne. I was sitting with you too. Jeet Singh and his wife were standing in front of us with folded hands. And they put their crowns on our heads.

Mota: Oh, foolish woman. How do bad feelings arise in your heart? Doesn't your nephew respect you despite being second in command after the queen? Doesn't he present every happiness of the world to you on your command? Then why did such evil come to your mind?

Do you want your husband's name and reputation to fall from the heights into the depths?

Wazirani: [In anger]What wrong have I done that you are fuming at me? I'm an idiot for telling you my dream. I thought your thinking is clear, just like mine. Who knew I would have to put up with so much scolding? Forgive me. I will neither tell you about my dream from today onwards nor should you scold me.

Mota: Dear, I didn't scold you. I was trying to make you think. The entire problem will suddenly spread like wildfire with only one word. You know how these things lead to issues.

Wazirani: But are you an outsider? Are you not a prince? Are you the son of a barber or a Brahmin? If he is ignorant about the kingdom, can you not become the king?

Mota: Keep quiet! Even the walls have ears. Now get ready, let's go to the palace. The king has called.

[CURTAINS]

Scene - 5

[Market of Jammu] [Two citizens come] First: *Jai Raghunathji!*

Second: *Jai Raghunathji!* Are you fine, brother?

First: Yes, brother

Second: You seem sad.

First: Brother, it's a matter of time.

Second: Yes, brother, our bad luck has shattered Jammu's greatness.

First: All this is the misdeed of that Mota. He has drowned the whole kingdom. Even in the last moments of King Ranjeet Dev, hc created a wedge between the father and son. This rascal has spoiled everything. Hey sinner, hope you get destroyed.

Second: Now people are saying that he is selling the kingdom to Ranjeet Singh.

First: Brother, it's a hundred percent true.

Second: Does King Jeet Singh speak at all?

First: What to talk about him? What will he say?

God has not given him such intelligence.

Second: Why won't somebody make him understand?

First: Has anyone ever learned from someone else's wisdom?

To whom God has given no wisdom, will he imbibe the wisdom provided to him?

What will the light of the lamp do for those whom God has blinded?

Even if an animal memorises the four *Vedas* and the six scriptures, it must carry the burden.

Kripa Sagar, why cry when you sow poison? Who will eat the lethal crop?

Second: Brother, you spoke right. Jeet Singh is a puppet and his cords are in the hands of the *wazir*. The king will dance as the *wazir* wishes.

First: The *wazir* has made him lazy by keeping him idle.

Second: Then how can he attain wisdom?

If you keep a hunting dog tied and fed, how will he be capable of hunting?

Although if he is fed leftovers and made to guard the sheep and goats, then he can even compete with wolves.

First: Brother, you spoke right. The king is the source of power, and if he becomes weak and worthless, then how will he rule?

Second: The king represents truth and purity, which translates to his subjects, making them truthful and pure.

First: A king is like the sun for his subjects. Just as the rays of the sun illuminate the world and make them feel powerful, the king too exudes light upon his subjects.

Second: Brother, what will happen to Duggar then?

First: What else will happen? The courtiers will keep fighting among themselves, and someone else will seize the opportunity.

Second: True. Only the nasty ones will create strife in the house. The clouds of *Kalyug* are wreaking havoc on our land as Ranjeet Singh is sitting at the border.

First: Enmity with Dido will come at a heavy cost to Mota. The whole country is with Dido.

Second: Nobody can find a person as brave as Dido!

First: Okay, Brother. Let's go from here. **[They leave]**

[CURTAINS]

Scene - 6

[Inside the Jammu Palace]

[The queen and her mother-in-law are sitting]

Queen: Oh, Mother! Look at Jammu's condition. See the state of this kingdom. There's no respect for the king. He is left as a toy in the *wazir's* hands.

Will he be like this his whole life? Will I always be on the receiving end of *Wazirani's* kicks? Did I get married to denigrate every queen?

Mother-in-law: No, dear. You are the queen of Jammu. No one can deny your order.

Queen: No, Mother! That's not the matter. When I was married, I thought like everyone else that the king would be a brave warrior, he would be skilful in speech, and I would also be respected. But my destiny is bad. All those wishes have only remained as dreams.

My body and heart started to burn to ashes at that point when I noticed that the monarch was constantly engaged in prayer, occasionally repeating the name of *God Ram* and counting beads like saints.

Mother-in-law: Daughter, prayers are not a bad thing.

Queen: But he prays all the time! Either he is the son of a Brahmin or of a Barber. It appears as though he has never seen a sword. The nearest thing to a battlefield for them is their backyard where they have only seen brass statues with a sword. What was the need for such a religious man to become the king? He should be a priest of *Raghunathji's* temple.

Mother-in-law: Daughter! Be patient. Everything will be fine at the right time.

Queen: It feels even worse when I go to the court. All the people blame the king. I don't mind the wazir, but what about Kishor Singh, Zorawar, Bishanaa, and Badhana? Everyone is so brilliant here, so what is the respect of the king in front of them?

Mother-in-law: Daughter! Everyone will step back.

Queen: Let them go to hell; it's none of my business. I'm too annoyed with the *Wazirani.* She has troubled me so much that I can't take it anymore! Her tantrums are too much to take. She walks in with her group of women, sits comfortably, and the women keep commenting on me. My heart tears to bits hearing their comments. Her tongue burns if she ever talks to me with a smile. Her accompanying women consider me a *Wazirani* and her as the queen of Jammu.

Mother-in-law: Daughter! Has the *Wazirani* ever been a queen?

Her ego is frail.

Queen: Mother! Why doesn't she boast? They have robbed the whole kingdom and filled their house. Then, why not make fun of our poverty? My heart wants to bruise her mouth. The day before yesterday, sitting with her friends, do you know what she was saying? She said her cheapest gowns were costlier than my father's whole kingdom.

Mother-in-law: Dear, do not pay heed to the comments made by filthy individuals.

[King Jeet Singh walks in]

Queen: Our good fortune! The great king has appeared. Did anyone break the string of your prayer beads? Or did the mice tear the *Vishnu's Sahasranama* pages to shreds?

[The king looks at her in disbelief.]

Queen: Come, sit down. Tell me why you have come here today.

King: [Being quiet for some time and then looking around, he asks if the *wazir* has not come yet.]

Queen: What is kept here for *wazir*? Why will he come here?

King: He will be coming

Queen: Must be to his own house.

King: No, he was saying he would come here.

Queen: Tell me, what is the matter?

King: He was saying, a great misery has befallen the kingdom.

Queen: Was he saying that, or do you think so?

King: He was saying.

Queen: He must be saying the time of happiness, not the misery. The kingdom may go to hell! They just want their *waziri* so that they can collect money from the people.

King: He was saying that Ranjeet Singh wants to grab the state.

Queen: And why does it matter to you? For you, praying at Raghunath's temple is enough. The *wazir* has already settled the state's work. The money in the treasury is just enough for the *Wazirani's* makeup. You are this kingdom's king only in title.

King: Why are you speaking ill of the *wazir*? Don't trust people's statements; they just make pigeons from the feathers. The *wazir* wishes well for us.

Queen: You think he is our well-wisher?

King: Of course!

Queen: You don't know his nature yet. Falsehood fills his veins. He has cut you from the roots, and you don't even realise that.

King: Listen, Love. If we know things clearly, where is the scope of doubt? He freed me from captivity and made me sit on the throne. It would be very ungrateful to forget his favour. How did he cut our roots? Can you tell me?

Queen: He killed your father and your brothers, he put you in prison, destroyed your *Kshatriya* qualities and governing instinct. What more harm can someone do than this?

[The *wazir* and *Wazirani* come]

Mota: Hail Great King!

King: *Jai Raghunath!* Come *Wazir,* sit.

[***Wazir*** sits near the king and ***Wazirani*** sits near the queen and her mother-in-law]

Mota: Great King! Ranjeet Singh's army has reached Puramandal. With his military, Kunwar Khadak Singh, war expert Diwan Mohakamchand, and Bhai Ram Singh, an officer of the information department, will arrive in Jammu today.

Now guide us: How do we get past these challenging times?

King: Let's think. Where is the other Wazir?

Mota: Great King, they are just arriving.

**[Badhana, Bishanaa, Dido,
Diwan Singh, and Bhupdev are coming]**

Mota: Wazirs, today our kingdom is in great trouble. What should we do? This time your efficiency, skill, and foresight can only save us. What can we do so that we don't get ourselves into a war and also so that the enemy doesn't attack us?

A kingdom that is void of rice and money

Whose servants have brought their king to his knees,

On whose border lurks the enemy,

Think hard and tell us:

Can we bring back our kingdom of gold and honey?

Bishanaa: Mr Wazir, you should see the condition of Chibb, Bahu, Chamba, Basoholi, and Kangada first, then you may strategise.

Diwan Singh: Brother Bishanaa, why do you name Chamba and Basohali? They are on one side and you are on the other. Now your courage and wisdom will be tested. Tell me. Are you ready to be tested?

Bishanaa: Brother, I'm with you all.

Badhana: Brothers, talk only about what is absolutely true and possible. Make sure the snake gets killed but the stave doesn't break.

Dido: Listen, it's good to be together. If all of us stand together, even if we lose, we will not be insulted.

Bishanaa: Can you defeat Ranjeet Singh?

Diwan Singh: Yes, if you end this antagonism between you two and if you are determined to give your life for the honour of the kingdom.

Dido: Ranjeet will not leave you until he is convinced that the hill people are as resolute as their land and are not going to stray from their purpose.

Badhana: Reconciliation won't work?

Diwan Singh: Brother, we know of your reconciliation. You reconciled with Maha Singh, and the city was still robbed. You reconciled with Brajraj, but they still attacked us.

Dido: They know that there is no unity among us and that we can behead each other for selfish motives.

Mota: You are talking about Maha Singh? There is a big difference between him and Ranjeet Singh. He was not a king, but Ranjeet Singh is. Earlier, he used to rule only over the inconsequential people, but now he rules the entire kingdom. He used to sign a treaty under duress, but Ranjeet Singh compromises to ensure comfort for the people.

Dido: What you say is right, but it is not good to be so terrified. If we are determined not to bear the subjection of Ranjeet Singh, then why fear him? Our Thakurians will bash him and sweep him away with a broom.

Mota: I believe in Mian Dido's bravery. But Ranjeet Singh is not what we think he is. Look towards Mandi, Suket, and Nadaun. The stones under the bushes there also repeatedly call for help. Do you want Tawi River to turn red with your blood? He doesn't think beyond dance, drama, and parties; he only wants to escape reality. Don't you know that to protect delicate plants from cold and fog, the gardener covers them with grass?

Bishanaa: If you see the great glory of Ranjeet Singh – like Nidhan Singh Panchhathha, Fula Singh Akali, Hari Singh Nalua, Mohakam Chand Diwan, Desa Singh Mijithiya, and Nihal Singh Atari Wala, many brave young men obey his orders.

Bhupdev: Uncle Bishanaa! If you're afraid of them, go and lock yourself in the inner hole of your house. Make sure they don't get caught. They haven't even left their house and you are trembling here out of fear.

Mota: Watch your language, Bhup. Younger ones should remain silent before the elders.

Bhupdev: I have understood the plan of our elders. They want us to die fighting, while they want to live. If I'm the son of Diwan Singh, then their intent will never be fulfilled.

Mota: Diwan Singh! Handle him.

Diwan Singh: Stop, Bhupu, control your tongue. Bishanaa, what did you mean by your comment?

Bishanaa: Whoever the enemy may be, we should be afraid of him. Ranjeet Singh is very prudent.

Diwan Singh: You have lost courage; what bravery will you show by going to the battlefield?

Queen: The king intends that the army should be ready to fight.

Mota: Your Highness, the king is intelligent. He can decide for himself. Women should not interfere in this work.

Queen: Well, if he was intelligent, why do you always try to become the chief?

Mota: Your Highness, I am not trying to act like a king, I'm a *wazir*. If he commands, I will even give up the position of *wazir*.

Bhupdev: Then why not leave? Take off your disguise. Since you have become the *wazir*, the kingdom has continuously deteriorated. You haven't even allowed the top officers to speak.

Diwan Singh: Brother, no one was happy with your *waziri.*

Bhupdev: To protect themselves from the Sikhs, people collected donations and gave gifts, but the city is still looted.

We gave compensation to them but still couldn't escape the loot of Punjab. Sometimes you and at other times they looted.

Dido: These days, the kingdom treasury is used for either the palace of the *wazir* or for the jewellery and clothing of the *Wazirani.* This is why people do not pay taxes.

Queen: Do you intend to sell the kingdom by taking a bribe from Ranjeet Singh?

Mota: Your Highness, you can say whatever you want. But if someone else says anything, then I will deal with them.

Dido: I am saying, come deal with me.

Mota: Do you have any evidence? **Dido:** Of course, I do.

Mota: Okay, I will talk to you. **[He leaves]**

[The queen hits the *Wazirani* hard with her fan.]

Queen: Hey, stupid! Can't you see the fan? Have you gone blind?

[Wazirani was surprised to see ***Wazirani's*** tearful eyes.]

Queen: Oh, God, it was you? I didn't notice.

Wazirani: [Red with anger] It is me! Oh, clever woman! Should I take your blindfold off?

King: [With folded hands] Aunty, Aunty, please don't blow up the matter. She didn't intentionally slap you.

Wazirani: Oh, she didn't? God is also afraid of seeing such a character. Oh my God! Get her treated in time. She knows every trick; you will dance to her commands. I won't call myself my father's daughter if I didn't avenge this slap.

Mother-in-law: Dear, leave it. You are older. She did not slap you intentionally.

Wazirani: God, give me the patience to bear this all. **[She leaves]**

Scene - 7

[King Ranjeet Singh arrives.]

King: [To himself.] *What to do? Jammu is uncontrollable so far. Deewan Mohakamchand did not send any news. He got busy with the bath at Puramandal and doesn't even go anywhere. We had said that we will finish the work of Jammu soon, but I don't know whom he was waiting for.*

Very well, call the Fakir.

Soldier: As you wish, Great King. **[He goes.]**

King: Brajraj Dev was our father's brother by relation. Both had exchanged their turbans. If he dies, then who becomes the king of the kingdom? People forcibly placed Jeet Singh on the throne. What was his right?

There is no right to the nephew. We are also nephews from the turban's relationship, and our right is more than his. When Brajraj Dev killed Dalel Singh and took over the throne, where did his son's right remain?

If I follow his wisdom, then he has no right. Therefore, it is our right to rule over Jammu.

[Fakir Ajijdeen comes]

King: Mr. Fakir! Any news from Jammu?

Fakir Ajijdeen: Respected king, Sangat Singh has just arrived. The Queen has sent a message for Kanwarji. She said, if he returns to the kingdom, she will give him the kingdom of Jammu.

King: Yes, it's great. Tell the *diwan* to meet the queen soon.

[Brother Ram Singh comes]

King: What news have you brought? Did *Diwan* meet the Queen?

Ram Singh: Great King, it feels like we have won Jammu. Mian Mota has called the *diwan* to Jammu for a meeting with him.

King: It's great. Tell the *diwan* that Mian Mota's Waziri should be intact. Ajeeb Singh Kalal should leave Gujrat and take over the charge of Jammu.

Ram Singh: As you wish, Great King.

[CURTAIN]

Scene - 8

Wazir's House

[Mota is sitting, Bishanaa comes]

Bishanaa: *Jai Wazirji*!

Mota: *Jai Bishanaa!* Have you proclaimed everywhere?

Bishanaa: Yes, *Wazirji*. I've proclaimed everywhere. The officials also served it. Mian Dido, Diwan Singh of Reasi state, his son Bhupdev, Dharam Singh Raipuria, and Shripat are seditious. Their estates are also confiscated.

Mota: Did anyone speak against it?

Bishanaa: Nobody spoke at that juncture. Maybe they are poisoning their minds.

Mota: Come, ask the temple's priest also to tell the people about their rebellion.

Bishanaa: Very good, King.

[He goes]

[Billa Pandit arrives]

Mota: *Panditji*, I touch your feet. Tell me, how come you're here?

Billa: Stay blessed, *Wazir*. I heard that you have seized the estates of people. That's bad.

Mota: *Panditji*, If I sting a lancet into an ulcer full of pus, then what is wrong with it? It is good for the patient.

Billa: *Wazirji*, I don't know this knowledge. Please, don't get angry, but the grass always appears greener on the other side of the fence. Is that province not a part of this kingdom?

Mota: Goitre is also part of the body. Who doesn't want it removed from the body? Similarly, for seditious people, even if they are our own, we must disown them.

Billa: Very well, then, whoever the world considers as an enemy is considered as bad no matter how righteous he is. Physical disorders like boils and goitre grow from inside. If they are treated well, why would they grow? You want to get Diwan Singh out of *Reasi* estate and keep Bishna there. What sin did Bhupdev commit that you are taking away his ancestral estate? What wrong did Dido do for you to confiscate his estate?

Mota: He wants to dethrone Jeet Singh. He has no right to live in his kingdom and say this! Should I have pretended not to hear this despite being a *wazir*?

Billa: *Wazir*, you are getting yourself into trouble by putting your hands in the wasp hive. All the good people of the kingdom are with them.

Mota: *Panditji*, irrespective of what happens, the estates of Dido, Bhupdev, and Shripatit will remain confiscated.

Billa: Okay *Wazirji*, do as you wish. May God bless, and may it be auspicious for all of us!

Don't know what will happen but I only know that good work has a good outcome and bad work has bad results.

[Leaves]

Scene - 9

[Maharaja Ranjit Singh's camp]
(Maharaj congratulates)

Maharaj: [To himself] *Now the fear of the mountains is over. Chamba, Bahosli, Kangda, Mandi, and Nadaun, administrators have been appointed everywhere. There is a widespread celebration of our victory. The soldiers too are celebrating at the camp. It is their right to celebrate after winning. The horses are in the stable, without the bridle, eating grains in excitement. Neither do they have a saddle on their backs, any sound of bigul, nor the riders to hit them and make them run. How fun is it there? The swords are closed in their sheaths. Guns, bullets, everything is left unused. After all the hard work, the mind is delighted and wants to fly in the open sky.*

[One Bhatt comes in and sings
a song worshipping Vishnu.]

Bhatt: In the primal time of creation, when Brahma appeared from the lotus, he created the *Chaturanan* who is superior to all. Thanks to God, all is your grace. Someone who infuses life into earthen moulds, who created nature from the mix of elements, who created from the tiniest organisms to giant animals, which are innumerable. Rules of the creation of nature, well-being of creatures,

Sin, virtue, and ritual: their division and upkeep. For destruction, Girijapati becomes Ish. Waves of Ganga flow from his tresses.

Grain, wind, water. Everything. Who created a world as worthy? God of Gods, Vishnu appears. Glory in Triloki which is sung in Vedas. Rule of this Trimurti in Triloki who has omniscient sight, origin of the universe, rearing, devastation, and annihilation of nature.

By his grace, kingships are bestowed in this world from his blessings. The rank of Trimurti is bestowed on kings.

Who nourishes the state and destroys the enemies? Whose scales of justice are equal?

Who arranges grains and who feeds the creatures? Such people are the hallmark of the State.

Where kings rule with religion and truth;

Self-governance is the strength of the state; Ranjit Singh, who takes such an ideal state

And then the custom of justice, which has prevailed in Punjab.

Respect of a gentleman and disrespect of evil Sacred lives have come to know life again. Expansion of Punjab in Kabul, Kandahar, Tibet, and Kashmir also, Punjab is exalted as an example. Kripa Sagar says, "Ranjit Singh, the world rises." The time will stand by the king of Punjab.

Maharaj: Where do you come from? What for? What do you want from us?

Bhatt: [Bends down]

You are blessed, Maharaj. You are very famous among the people in this kingdom. Those who stand against you are foolish and will surely die. You have fulfilled the wishes of everyone who came to your door. May your treasure always be filled with the grace of God. I came here to ask only a bit from that treasure.

Maharaj: Give him 500 Rupees and some food.

Beggar: Thank you, Good Lord.

Bhatt: [Again bent down]

You are the true king. Live long. What the ears had heard, the eyes saw. Hindu-Muslim all are equal to you. Sitting on the throne of religion, you have had fun. You have helped everyone and brought a smile to everyone's face, and this is the true achievement of my king.

King: Okay, okay. Bloody rich people, you just have to beg and give excuses.

Bhatt: [Again bows down]

Great King, you have only one auspicious eye, whereas people with two eyes bow down or salute.

Great King: [Laughing] Go, set free the horse from the stable. Bloody rich people. Do you want to enrol in the cavalry?

Bhatt: Great King! Make me *kumedan*.

[King laughs]

Beggar: Take, good man, this letter to the treasury.

[Priest goes with the letter]

Great King: [To the beggar] Did you have any work?

Beggar: Great King, Mota has sent some men.

Great King: Where are they? Bring them before me. **[The beggar orders the men to come in front]**

Beggar: Great King! He is Kishor Singh, the brave son of Mian Mota's.

Great King: He is so beautiful and young. Brother, have you ever gone to war?

Kishor Singh: Yes, when you attacked Jammu, I fought your army.

Great King: Who is this boy with you?

Kishor Singh: Great King! This is my elder son, Gulab Singh.

Great King: This young man too exudes bravery. Has he ever gone to war?

Gulab Singh: Great King! I was a servant of Sardar Nihal Singh. It was I who showed prowess at Sang's fort.

Great King: Do you know Diwan Khushvakat Rai?

Gulab Singh: Yes, Great King! I fought on their behalf.

Great King: Will you do an army job?

Gulab Singh: What should be a better job for someone who is a soldier by birth?

Great King: *Jamadarji*, hire the father and his son on five Rupees of daily wage each. They will stay with *Divan* Mohkam Chand.

Jamadar: Noted, Great King!

Beggar: Great King, he is Dhyan Singh, a soldier younger than Gulab Singh.

Great King: Even though he is younger, he seems to have a good mind. Place him at the main gate. Give him two Rupees daily.

Jamadar: As you order, Great King!

Beggar: Great King, this is Suchet Singh; he also wants to serve.

Great King: Place him alongside Jamadar. Give him one Rupee daily.

[CURTAINS]

Scene - 10

[At the Police Station of Jammu]

[Kotwal is sitting]

Kotwal: Two strong guards are needed in the city. Bring men of use for the work.

Ardali: Lord, two men have come to see you.

Kotwal: Bring them in.

[The men come]

Kotwal: [Has a look at them.] Listen, Brother, we need pure and trustworthy men.

Sarban: Lord, you can count on us! We have worked in Shah's stable for two months and at a wine shop for six months. You can't find a better servant than us. You can ask anyone you want.

Kotwal: Okay, okay. I understand. You are men of your word.

Ardali: Lord, they will go to hell if they are not loyal.

Kotwal: Well then. Tell them their duties.

Ardali: So, the one among you with a dry disposition, a clean heart, and a stone-like strong heart, will be made *jamadar.*

Nihala: I am, I am! I have studied up to the third grade.

Kotwal: Wow, Nihal Wow! God has given you great looks too. But listen, Nihal, beauty is rare. Everyone knows how to read and write.

Nihala: Kotwalji, I can do both.

Kotwal: I know that you know. Thank God for your face and form. The blend of the two is rare. But reading and writing isn't bravery. It is only a show-off. Bring this out only when it is necessary.

Ardali: If you want to become a good jamadar, stand silently. Take this lantern. You must keep a watch on the men who roam freely.

Sarban: If I see such a man, what do I do?

Ardali: What to do? Tell him to stop.

Sarban: And if he doesn't halt?

Ardali: So what? Don't care about him. Just think you have avoided an unnecessary confrontation.

Kotwal: If he doesn't halt, understand that he is not the subject of the great king.

Sarban: Okay, we must guard the king's personnel; why do we need to think about the others?

Ardali: Don't make loud sounds in the lanes. People must be sleeping and won't want the guard to make noise.

Sarban: Why will we make noise? We will be asleep.

Ardali: You seem like an old, experienced guard, the one that sleeps. What harm can an old guard do to anyone? But see to it that nobody snatches the lantern away.

Sarban: Okay! We will keep it close to our chest.

Ardali: Also, go around the wine shop and see if you find any drunkards. Ask them to go home and sleep.

Sarban: And if he doesn't go?

Ardali: Then let him lie there. If he can't answer your questions appropriately, then he is of no use.

Sarban: Got it.

Ardali: If you find a thief, or suspect someone, you can question them. But try to avoid men like these as much as possible if you want to gain the respect of others.

Nihala: If we know for sure that he is a thief, should we catch him or not?

Ardali: Why not? You may catch him. But if you get into the mud, your own clothes will be stained. Firstly, he must prove himself as a thief. If he steals someone's slipper, turban, or lantern, only then can you catch him; otherwise, why would you catch him without proof?

Nihala: Yes! Why catch without proof?

Ardali: Nihalchand, your comprehension is excellent.

Nihala: Even dogs should not be hanged forcibly; ultimately even the thief is human.

Ardali: Mian Nihal, you are so understanding. You may become a *Jamadar.*

Sarban: And?

Ardali: At night, if a child cries, then ask his mother or maid to silence him.

Sarban: And what if she doesn't listen to us?

Ardali: Then what? Ignore it and walk away. The child will stop by itself after repeated weeping. If the goat doesn't understand the *'baa'* of her kid, why would she understand the *'moo'* of a calf?

Nihala: How thoughtful.

Ardali: Yes, the job is yours. You are a government representative. While doing your duty, if you find someone from the government doing wrong, you can also question him.

Sarban: I don't believe it; this is a lie!

Ardali: Let's have a bet of five Rupees. We can stop them if that's in the favour of the government, but if we do it against the will of our government, then it is a crime. A guard should not commit any sort of crime.

Nihala: I already know this.

Ardali: Okay! Now, take charge. If any problem arises, come to me. Consult with each other. Ask the neighbours also.

Sarban: Yes, we understand.

[He leaves]

Kotwal: Take your charge, we are going.

[He leaves]

Sarban: We have understood our job. Come now, sit there.

Nihala: Let's take a nap. We'll wake up later.

Sarban: Okay.

[They both sleep and start snoring]

Dido: [Dido comes] These soldiers of Jammu are snoring on duty!

[He pokes them with the hilt of the sword.]

Guard: [Waking up nervously] We are guards.

Dido: You, bloody guards! Why are you sleeping?

Guard: We were awoken from inside.

[Dido slaps, Soldiers shiver]

Dido: Then guard like professionals, or else I will snatch the lantern!

[The guards reposition themselves and Dido leaves]

Guard: Thank God, he didn't snatch our lantern, otherwise we would lose our jobs.

[CURTAINS]

Part II

Scene - 1

[Dense Forest]

[Dido comes with a hawk in his hands]

Dido: [Sings to himself]

A dead creature hiding in some corner.

Who has neither passion in mind, nor a fire in their heart.

That this is my country, a place where I was born.

There is my welfare in the holy dust of this earth. In whose mind, no anger of any kind arises.

When you want to move towards your homeland by roaming anxiously in a foreign land.

Go, test if there is such a creature who is living without a cause; he is a burden on earth.

A poet will not sing a melody after suffering from something.

A black heart will bring dark emotion in the dark. Even if the aim was high to achieve the kingdom's high status.

The robber's clan had also named it big. There is no dearth of anything, delusion is according to desire.

The ruler made a great warrior whose shadow scares people.

If he became too dishonest, he would only gather wealth.

Around this idyll, the status will pull the curtain. He loses glory and beauty while alive.

If a dies a double death, it drops down with a thud towards bad soil, in which he takes birth.

In whose name, no work becomes glorious.

Who pricks the boil-like Earth with a lancet?

Then why regret, mourn, and cry at his goodbye.

[Thakurian comes]

Thakurian: Great King! Why have you left home and are wandering alone here? There is sadness on your face. You are a brave warrior! Whom do you fear so much that is so strong?

Dido: Dear! I am processing some suppressed grief. You know the pure land of Duggar, my motherland, the birthplace of Maaldev, Hamirdev, Dhruvdev, and Ranjitdev in which thousands of warriors gained fame in this world? Right now, this land is under the grip of the robbers. This flowing water of Tawi, that used to please our mind, has now become filthy due to the misdeeds of the outsiders.

Thakurian: Dear husband, this world is constantly in motion.

Nothing lasts forever; so why are you doubting yourself?

Dido: Your Majesty, I don't doubt but look, the Sun God still rises as before. It accentuates the beauty of the mountains. But now his splendour doesn't give me happiness but only brings sorrow to my heart. This bright-looking moon that's smiling playfully cuddles, loves, and pampers the hills. It does not give me respite or peace but makes my mind impatient.

Thakurian: Great King! You seem fascinated. Come back to your senses. Your spirit will fly high in the sky because it is nourished by the warrior clan. Why are you moving towards fascination?

Dido: Dear wife, there is a difference between the sky and the land. Although, at this time, I make fun of subjugation, but I fear it. With every passing day, the pain and fear are growing.

Thakurian: You are absolutely free in this open courtyard of Goddess Trikuta. The whole Duggar respects you. There is no shortage of money and grain. Brave warriors are waiting for your command. Then what are you lacking?

Dido: You tell me. If someone's house catches fire and flames reach the sky, can the snow of the Himalayas cool it down? If the stomach is empty, can the thought of a wedding party by a rich person fill the belly? Never! It will hurt the soul even more.

[Looking outside] Hey Duggar! I will sacrifice myself for you.

[Bhupdev comes]

Bhupdev: Tell, Brother. What to do now?

Dido: Tell me, how is Jammu?

Bhupdev: Brother, Punjabis took over the kingdom.

Dido: Mote, you evil soul. Go away!

Bhupdev: Ajit Singh Kalal became a working officer.

Motu is the *wazir*, but all the power lies with the working officer.

Dido: Damn this *waziri*! Getting insulted by everyone is not the job of a *wazir*.

Bhupdev: Then what to do?

Dido: Ask Motu to leave the *waziri*. We will deal with Punjab ourselves.

Bhupdev: Will he leave? If a dog grows fond of a bone, he won't leave it.

Dido: Ask the Sikhs to take away Motu's Waziri.

Bhupdev: Why will they do that? An insider can cause the maximum damage just like a small leak can sink the whole ship. And Motu Dogra is the handle of the Punjabi's axe with which they will cut off the Duggar roots.

Dido: Brother, that's what I am saying. Kill Motu! If an infected finger isn't getting better even after treatment, amputating that finger is the only cure.

Bhupdev: I am also saying this, but it is important to consult the queen.

Dido: Okay, where is she?

Bhupdev: The queen has gone to Jaganaur's estate.

Dido: Okay, let's go to her and we will talk in detail.

[They leave]

Scene - 2

[Jaganaur's state]

[The queen arrives]

Queen: What I feared has happened. Mian Mota, the evil mind, messed up the kingdom. Thankfully, at least the estate is saved for me to sigh in relief. Now what? We still have many loyal devotees. But what might happen tomorrow? Dido, Bhupdev, and Dharm Singh are our assets! The whole kingdom is with them. God bless us!

[Dido and Bhupdev come.]

Guard: Veer Dido and Bhupdev have come.

Queen: What's the news?

Dido: Great Queen, the whole country is with us. The family of Billa Pandit, Shripat Dhandi, Dharm Singh Rapuria, Chain Singh of Hansali, Mian Chhano, and numerous warriors are ready to sacrifice their lives.

Queen: That's great. Now, what should we do?

Dido: First, kill Mota.

Bhupdev: We will not leave Mota alive.

Dido: He is the primary divisive force. As long as he is alive, he will divide our companions.

Bhupdev: But if he is no longer leading the force, who will kill the Punjabis?

Queen: You are right. But killing Mota might not work. We will get trapped in a bigger mess and the real work will be left unfinished.

Dido: Killing Mota will have a good effect. The Punjabis will be scared of us.

Queen: Okay, brave Dido. I am with you.

Bhupdev: Keep this plan a secret. Take care.

Queen: Don't worry about me. Who will take this responsibility?

Dido: We need a mercenary.

Bhupdev: Someone who hides their bad intentions behind the veneer of friendliness.

Dido: Someone who is stone-hearted. On whom mercy and sympathy have no effect.

Bhupdev: I know two such people. You can call them and talk.

Dido: Who are they?

Bhupdev: Satru and Triddu.

Queen: Yes, I know, they are the men of use.

Dido: Call them and talk.

Queen: [To servant] Hey, Ghasitu, come here.

[Ghasita comes]

Go, call both Satru and Triddu.

[Ghasita goes]

Dido: How will these people work?

Queen: When Mota will be returning home in evening, they will find him on the way?

Bhupdev: Absolutely right.

[Satru and Triddo come]

Dido: Satru, are you fine? How are you, Triddu?

Satru: Good Sir, give us your order.

Dido: Satru, you are our good friend. We have always had a brotherly relationship with Triddu and you.

Bhupdev: Satru, you are our neighbours. You are from my caste and clan. I need your help if you will agree.

Satru: What to do, Lord? If we won't help you, then whom will we help?

Dido: The job is not easy; it must be executed with great intelligence.

Satru: Okay, what is it?

Dido: Just keep this in your heart. Nobody should be aware of this.

Satru: Why would anyone be aware of this? Are we such men?

Triddu: We are official men. Not common people.

Dido: Yes, I know, Triddu, that you are a professional.

Satru: *Thakurji*, we are from a reputed family. You have my word.

Dido: Okay, Satru. You know that Punjab has conquered the kingdom of Duggar.

Satru: Yes, when I went to the court that day, there were a lot of fireworks.

Dido: These fireworks mean Dogras are no longer useful.

Satru: Okay, nobody told me this. Had I known it, I would have beaten those who lit the fireworks.

Dido: Okay, now you know. Tell us, who is behind this state of Duggar?

Satru: Destiny, Maharaja, destiny.

Dido: Wow, Satru! A brave man like you is crying before destiny! This answer of yours broke all my expectations. Listen, destiny is not anything. This is just a word made by a coward. Lazy people don't move their hands and feet and hide the voice of their soul. Behind the bad state of Duggar lies our laziness and cowardice.

Satru: If so, then this will be the case.

Triddu: Until I do not rob someone's house, my condition will remain bad. Then where is the luck?

Dido: Well done, Triddu. You understand it well.

A hardworking man should not even mention the name of destiny.

Satru: I understand. When we broke into the house of Belishah and killed the caretaker, people used to say it was the destiny of Belishah. And I said, "We are the destiny of Belishah!"

Dido: Now, you understand.

Satru: I said, now there is not a little doubt. A man's destiny is in his own hands.

Dido: Now tell me, who tore Duggar to tatters?

Satru: I said, "People, Great King!"

Dido: Tell me, which man from Duggar brought Punjabis to Jammu?

Satru: Mian Mota, our elder brother, will fight alongside the Punjabis.

Dido: Satru, now you understand well. He is not our elder to be respected. he is the one who sold his country to the Punjabis.

Satru: Oh, Lord! I understood. I will never call him my elder brother now.

Dido: Triddu! Do you understand?

Triddu: Lord! I know well that you always talk sensibly.

Dido: Do you know the treatment such people receive?

Satru: The same that boils full of pus.

Dido: Well done, Satru, you speak intelligently.

Triddu: Lord! We are the servants of the king.

Queen: So be ready. Make your heart strong. When he leaves the court, fire the gun at him. When he falls unconscious, cut his head off with the sword. The evening darkness will hide you. Take these two hundred Rupees and we will give four hundred Rupees once you bring us his head.

Satru: Your wish is our command, Great Queen.

Queen: Go with your covered face and don't speak.

Satru: I know, Lord! Whoever talks more does no work.

Triddu: We will use our hands, not tongues.

Queen: Good. Brace yourself!

Triddu: Okay, we will go well-prepared.

Dido: Go, may the Almighty be with you.

Both: Good Lord!

[They go]

Scene - 3

[Village Courtyard]

Chatthi: [Leaving house] Hey sisters! If someone has a mortar, give it to me. I have to pound the paddy.

Hanjara: [Coming out] Sister Chatthi, you should wait for the day to rise. People are preparing breakfast and now you're bringing the paddy.

Chatthi: Sister, what can I do being alone? If someone were with me for help, I would make breakfast like you too.

Hanjara: Why don't you ask Khadku's father to get the rice out of the machine?

Chatthi *Shree Ram! Shree Ram!* Khadak Singh's father never gets anything done. He is always fastened to the peg. Whether to grind wheat or extract rice. I have to do everything.

Hanjara: Sister, my husband is good; if I say anything, he immediately does it.

Chatthi: If this is the case, then why should I regret it?

Hanjara: Sister, you are great. I can't handle this mess.

Chatthi: Nobody helps. If I don't work, then who will help me? Look, the sun is shining on our heads. I have to sift rice and prepare breakfast. From where can I get a mortar, do you have any idea?

Hanjara: It is like that adage. The girl is next to you, but you are drumming in the city. Take from your neighbour, Chimi, but don't tell her my name.

Chatthi: [Visiting Chimi's courtyard]

Chimi, hey Chimi. Why don't you speak?

Chimi: [From inside] Yes, dear.

Chatthi: How long do I have to wait for the mortar? Have you put cotton in your ears? Even if I die shouting, you will not hear me.

Chimi: Oh, I swear I didn't hear anything. I was making whey. Mortar is in Badaich's house. She hasn't returned it yet. I had to pound rice. Gyan's father didn't even bring it back.

Chatthi: Oh God! Now I must go to Badaich's house? Is Gyan at home or not? Tell him to go.

Chimi: Is a mortar brought by such a little child? But if Gyan's father had been at home, he would have done you that favour.

Chatthi: Sister, these men have troubled us a lot. They are not worried about salt, turmeric, or anything! Even if the house goes to hell, they'll just sit to eat the cooked food.

Chimi: Yes, dear. Nobody listens to us. If we say something, they get annoyed. And yes, they'll work only when they are in a good mood.

Chatthi: Sister, this is the condition in every house. See now, I must pound the paddy and then I have to make breakfast. Children are hungry.

Chimi: Dear, go and ask Jumme Harijan to go to Badaich's house.

**[Mouja Singh comes with his dog,
with a gun on his shoulder, a bag around
his neck, wearing a turban on his head
and some hair sticking out of his turban.]**

Mouja Singh: [To his dog] Moti, Moti, come here soon, beautiful.

Chatthi: [On seeing him] Hey, Mouja Singh. Well done.

Mouja Singh: [He standup and laugh]

Chatthi: You came to me in a moment of need; I really needed you.

Mouja Singh: [Chirps]

Chimi: See, God helps those who help themselves.

Chatthi: I will be very grateful to you, Mouja Singh, if you do me a favour. But before that, drink this whey.

[She leads him, holding his hand. Mouja Singh continues to chuckle, shaking his shoulders.]

Chatthi: [Chatthi brings a glass of whey with extra butter.] Good, drink it.

[Mouja Singh drinks quickly.]

Chatthi: Brother, bring me the mortar from Badaich's house. I'm pleading with everyone, but no one is going to bring it.

Mouja Singh: Badaich's house? But it is miles away.

Chatthi: Miles, yeah. Four miles away. Is it far for a young man like you? Go fast, my brother.

Chimi: Oh, go sly. She has been pleading for a long time. If the brother-in-law does not work for his sister-in-law, then who will?

[Mouja Singh flips his shoulders and goes away looking with widened eyes.]

Chatthi: Well done, my good brother. **[She shouts from behind.]** Hey, come soon.

[Mouja Singh carries the mortar on his back and leaves it in Chatthi's courtyard.]

Chatthi: Come inside, young man, and bring your sister-in-law along to take out some rice by tamping the paddy. I've made breakfast; you can also eat with us.

[Chatthi is to put paddy in the mortar and Mouja Singh tamp it]

Mouja Singh: [After tamping] Now clean it by yourself.

Chatthi: My good brother. Now don't leave work halfway. The bamboo winnowing tray is hanging inside the room with the peg, please bring it.

Mouja Singh: Take the rice.

Chatthi: [On seeing the rice] Wow, Mouja Singh! You are too good at this.

Nanda: [Leaving home] Has anyone seen Mouja Singh here?

Chimi: There he is! Taking out rice for Chatthi.

Nanda: [From far away]Wow, Mouja Singh! I've been waiting for so long. Please pass by my house.

Mouja Singh: Why?

Nanda: Some maize is kept for grinding, brother. Please help me with it.

Mouja	Singh:	Where is that maize?
Nanda:		Look at our furnace here.
Mouja	Singh:	Bring it to me for grinding. **[Nanda brings a pot full of maize and keeps it nearby.]**

Nanda:		Do it quickly. God bless you.
		I'm making *makki toda* for you. I will also give it to Moti.
Mouja	Singh:	**[After grinding all the maize from the pot, he cleans his hands and feet.]** Take it, everything is done.
Nanda:		**[After seeing flour]** The flour is so good. Mouja Singh, you are simply great at this work. Now please eat the hot maize bread. Do you like greens or turnips?
Mouja	Singh:	Greens! [Nanda gives a thick bread of maize and a bowl full of greens. Mouja Singh eats.]
Mouja	Singh:	Sister-in-law, Nanda, the greens are very tasty.
Nanda:		I picked the softest greens from the fields. [Do you want more?]
Mouja	Singh:	Give me one more spoon.
		[Nanda gives another bowl of greens.]
Rupa:		**[Coming to the courtyard]**Has Mouja Singh come here?

Mouja Singh: [On seeing Rupa] What is it?

Rupa: Take my boy out to play. Ever since his father left the house, he keeps crying and acts stubbornly. Go out with him and show him the rooster.

Mouja Singh: [After stretching and belching] Let them sit on my shoulder.

Rupa: [To her son] Now this uncle will swing you.

[Rupa sits her son on Mouja Singh's shoulder.]

Jounsa: [Comes running] Hey, Mouja Singh. Now I'm distributing your burden equally. Take my Santo too with you.

[Jounsa puts her children over Mouja Singh's shoulder.]

Bhanno: Hey, everyone's kids will swing, so why won't my baby swing? Take my Tunde also on your shoulder.

Mouja Singh: Bhanno! Put him also on my shoulder from the back.

[Bhanno places her children over the shoulder of Mouja Singh.]

[Mouja Singh's wife, Bainti, comes holding a scoop in her hand. Along with her comes Mouja Singh's son, Fouja Singh, wearing long and loose pyjamas. He holds his pyjamas with one hand and with the other the loose end of his mother's saree and comes limping.]

Bainti: Wait! May everything of yours be destroyed. You must have nothing with you. Now you are carrying all of these children? Useless man. He has become everyone's horse. There is no concern for the land nor care for the animals. Neither care for home nor children. My life was ruined by my marriage. He continues to be at their service for all four sessions.

Rupa and [In anger] Bainti, behave yourself.

Jounsa: Do you have any manners?

Bainti: I know all of you who know how to talk with manners. They teach me ways to talk. The pain you all are having is well-known to me.

Jounsa: Why will I have a problem? May the almighty bring bad luck to you and your family!

Rupa: Don't disturb us, sister. We cannot compete with you.

Bainti: Yes, I'm a very argumentative person, and you are going to be silent.

But yes, if your husband is so worthless that everyone calls him nasty outside the house, what is your fault?

Mouja Singh: [Stares at her with the boys in his arms.]

Fouja Singh: Tries to climb onto his mother's shoulder.

Rupa: Do you want to share something with us?

Bainti: You all spoiled my house; now what is left to share?

Jounsa: Don't be angry, Bainti. By fighting, you have degraded this helpless person's intelligence.

Mouja Singh: [Keeps staring]

Bainti: Someone says it right. Only one person, and no one else, is aware of who suffers the most. This is a family man's predicament, right? Neither would he have married me nor gotten me into trouble. He always stays in the service of his sisters-in-law.

Mouja Singh: [Still keeps staring]

Chimi: Look, how good he is. Don't scold him. He has done no harm to you.

Bainti: Yes, Sister. If you don't get angry, who else should? Throughout the day, you keep him busy. If he is doing household work, why should I worry? See how Chimi and Chitthi thug, eat, and drink heavily but destroy others jointly.

Chimi: Hey! Mind your language. Do not call people a thug without proof. Your mouth is working a bit too much; you have no restraint! Your mother is a thug!

[Looks away and says] This quarrelsome woman has come early in the morning and started fighting.

Bainti: Me? You are quarrelsome and some people close to you. **[She says, hinting at Chatthi.]** You are all such obnoxious women that even trouble bystanders.

Chatthi: You don't fight us by screaming so much. No one is born yet to give you a brain. Such a gorgeous young guy has entered the latter stages of his life because of your habit.

[Bainti angrily charges toward Mouja Singh with the scoop.]

Bainti: Just wait. I will teach you a lesson today. You harass me and insult me before these women!

The women: Hey, someone, please come and save him from her!

[They all grab Bainti. All the villagers gather. Two or three people drive Mouja Singh away from there.]

Chanda Singh: [The head of the village comes]

Why is it so noisy? Everyone, go back to your home. Do you all think this is a wrestling ring?

[The women quickly go into the house.]

Chanda Singh: Bainti, what is all this?

Bainti: Chief, please ask these women who have together pushed me into this trouble.

Chanda Singh: Why did you come here?

Bainti: I came here to cry over my fate. The father of the children had gone at the crack of dawn and these women kept giving him work. Now they ask me, why I stop him. These quarrelsome women won't quit bothering me.

Chanda Singh: Bainti, no one should say such a wrong thing to anyone! See, everyone is sitting quietly in their house and you are calling them quarrelsome.

Bainti: Chief, only those suffering the plight know what it feels like. These women have destroyed my house. If I complain about them, they follow me like mad dogs. They do not encourage him to pursue the right path; instead, they give him refuge and watch the show.

Chanda Singh: Because you are idle? If a man does wrong, he must be shown the right path. Where has that idiot gone? **[Chanda Singh and Bainti look around but Mouja Singh is missing.]**

Bainti: He was still here. Don't know where he disappeared! The sisters-in-law must have hidden him somewhere.

Chanda Singh: Okay. You go home and handle the kids. I'll see him today. Useless! Worthless! Doesn't do any good.

Bainti: Chandaji, he has ruined so much property. He has no sentimental ties to the house. All day he spends time talking or playing here and there. If someone starts talking to him, he goes with them. I have to request people to sow crops on my land from where I get barely enough to feed myself. You are smart, the head of the village. Yet even you didn't give him any advice.

Chanda Singh: I learned of this today. Now look how I deal with them. Now you go home and please keep calm.

[Bainti goes away]

[CURTAINS]

Scene - 4

[Market]

[The shopkeepers are sitting. Some are smoking hookah, some are weighing goods while someone is cutting the thread. When Shivu Arora arrives.]

Gandhu: [He is wrapping the rope] Hey, Shiv Dayal! What happened to you? You no longer have any traces of a youthful guy in you. You are getting weaker day by day.

Rama: [Weighing the stuff] Gandhu, you don't know; Shivu got married.

Gandhu: Really?

Shivu: [Smiling]What did you see that made you smile?

Gandhu: Did I miss something? Where is your look, style, and that beautiful turban on your head? Now you look like a sick person.

Rama: Hey, Gandhu, are you crazy? When the burden of the household and family falls on your shoulders, you are left looking like this.

Gandhu: *Hey, Ram!* It seems like she is not a wife, she is a typhoon. Brother Shivu, is she really a typhoon? You need to man up.

Shivu: Brother, but I'm the same as before.

Rama: Are you kidding me? You seem a lot different than before. Where is that stubbornness now?

Shivu: Wisdom also changes as you grow older.

Gandhu: Ramdayal! Now he is studying with a new master.

Rama: Gandhu, you are right. In your whole life, you cannot possibly learn as much as your wife does in one day. The elders have said that qualities like love, a soft nature, patience, temperament, and sociability are found in a man who lives with a wife of strict nature.

Gandhu: Brother Shivdayal, is it okay? Even those with a short fuse are softened by their wife's stinging fire. This sermon truly is the finest in the entire world.

Kesar: Each woman should be treated respectfully and as the best creation of God, even if she has some anger issues.

Rama: Yes. What is the lie in this? Look a little towards Mouja Singh.

[Everyone is laughing]

Shivu: Wow, brother Rama, you consider me to be on par with Mouja Singh.

Gandhu: Not now, but you will definitely become someone someday.

Rama: Hey, you know whom you are talking about. He is a godly man, a perfectly calm man. He is down to earth. He eats whatever he gets without complaining about it. But Bainti does not let him rest and is after him all the time. She never stops belittling him. Even if he speaks a little, she scolds him so much that he becomes hapless and sits down silently.

Gandhu: Ouch! Yes! Yes, brother, then it is very fun. What answer should we give then?

It gives me inner peace when I see him in this condition where he is speechless and all he is able to do is stare blankly with his eyes wide open. All this infuriates Bainti even more, and she starts screaming at the top of her voice. All he can do at this moment is inhale and exhale deeply.

Rama: Hey, you know what happened with his dog, Moti? As soon as he goes to the courtyard of the house, he puts down his head, tucking his tail between his legs, and looks at Bainti. Then she picks up a ladle or a broom, and Moti runs for his life, whining.

Gandhu: Listen, Shivdayal, this is going to be the same with you.

Shivu: Brother, she will become intelligent herself when she gets older.

Rama: Hey, don't live in any delusions. The bitterness of the tongue increases with age. The sharpness of the tongue is such a weapon that the more you use it, the sharper it will be.

[Mouja Singh comes with a boy in his arm.]

Gandhu: Now, Mouja Singh has also come. Wow, Mouja Singh.

Mouja Singh: [Looks at them and keeps the boy down.]

Kesar: Today, Brother escaped from the clutches of death. He is lucky that he survived. Otherwise, he would remember being battered by that ladle for life.

[Mouja Singh looks happy.]

Karamchand: Then how did he survive?

Kesar: We reached the spot and pulled it out of the burning fire.

Gandhu: Is the fire extinguished now? Did the wooden scoop burn? Eventually, he will go home.

Kesar: Now all is well. Thank God! The bad time has also passed. When that time comes again, we will be there for you. Am I right, brother Mouja Singh? You may just laugh if you agree.

[Mouja Singh looks at him and chuckles lightly.]

Kesar: If we were not there today, Mouja Singh, you would not have been alive. Take this bundle to the mill.

[Mouja Singh picks up the bundle and goes towards the mill.]

[CURTAINS]

Scene - 5

[Mill]

[The mill man sits on the seat.]

Mill Man: Come, my ox, be fast. Grind the grains forty *maan.*

Gram, wheat, corn, maize. Who came, go across.

Sweat through day and night

Eat your food by taste

Live in a world of two days

Do something for the future, friend. Come, my ox, walk, walk, walk.

Don't stop even for a moment.

The work that God gave Let's go and never defer. Come, come, let's go.

The whole world is pacing up. This life is going on.

If you take advantage of life

Keep going even when afraid.

It is the mud from which a lotus arises.

Doing work is your right. Giving fruits is God's work.

Let's go, life goes on continuously. Don't keep the wish of fruit in the heart.

Walk, my ox, my magnanimous

Take the pleasure of life.

[Mouja Singh comes]

Mill Man: Mouja Singh! Where do you come from?

Mouja Singh: It comes from Kesar.

Mill Man: Wow, Mouja Singh! **[Sits on the seat.]** I will first eat food and then grind your grains.

[Mouja Singh on the seat.]

[Coming from inside.] We are blessed today.

Millman's wife: Mouja Singh has come.

[Mouja Singh stares and laughs.]

Come, I will do your work, you will do mine.

Millman's wife: [Mouja Singh quickly gets off the seat.]

Millman's wife: Take this one rupee, my good brother. Bring bundles of dry wood from Rajji's house. It is difficult for me to heat the oven. Go, bring

more.

[Mouja Singh goes and brings a big bundle.]

Millman's wife: Wow, my good brother, go and keep this

behind.

[Mouja Singh keeps]

Millman's wife: Take this flour and put it in a sack, then your grains will grind.

[Mouja Singh put the flour]

Millman's wife: Bring them, now I will grind your grains.

Mouja Singh: [Puts the bundle into the mill]

[Boys come from outside seeing Mouja Singh.]

Boys: Mouja Singh! Oh, Mouja Singh! Come play horse-horse.

Mouja Singh: [Gets out quickly]

A boy: [Holding his arm.] Give us a ride.

Another boy: Come here

[Mouja Singh goes.]

All: Walk my horse.

[They jump over.]

One boy: Brother, the first turn is mine. Mouja Singh, be a horse.

**[Mouja Singh becomes a horse,
all boys ride on his back, one by one.]**

One boy: [Comes running] Bainti is coming! Bainti is coming! She is holding a big stick in her hand. **[Everyone runs away]**

[CURTAINS]

Scene - 6

A Lane in Jammu

[Two people enter with covered mouths and heads]

Satru: I said, let's attack him from behind.

Triddu: No, friend. Tomorrow he will say they tried to kill me in deceit. We are respectful people; we don't want to be notorious.

Satru: If he lives, only then will he say.

Triddu: But you will wonder why you killed an innocent.

Satru: No, I will not.

Triddu: Friend, my mind has become unstable. **Satru:** Wow, you are just scared. But this is what we need to do.

Triddu: I am not scared of death because it is the queen's order.

Satru: I used to believe that you are strong at heart.

Triddu: I am strong, but I am afraid of sin.

Satru: Go, then return the advance to the Queen.

Triddu: Be patient. I know that my mind will be ready. Just think for a moment. It just takes the time it does to count all the way to twenty.

Satru: [After counting to twenty.] Now, is your mind stable or not?

Triddu: I swear on *Guruji*. We are not the same. We still have some differences left.

Satru: We will get 400 Rupees! 400!

Triddu: I swear, I had forgotten that. My mind is clear now.

Satru: I said, now tell me what is on your mind?

Triddu: For now, only the coins.

Satru: When she opens the box to give the reward, where will your mind be?

Triddu: Let it be, don't get rid of it.

Satru: If this mind changes again, then what will happen?

Triddu: Really, this is very bad. Now, I won't care about this.

Satru: I said, "Why?"

Triddu: This mind makes a man coward. It doesn't allow stealing. This shameless thing quickly decides that a man is a sinner; that a man can never abuse; that he can't stare at another woman. It quickly makes a man embarrassed. It keeps rousing the heart all the time; it is very stubborn. Once I found a purse full of coins; it made me return it.

Whoever believed it, it makes him a pauper. Do you know why great men do not allow it to come near them? Because it is of no use to them. Only the poor listen to its voice. I know only one thing, if a good man wants a happy life, then he must believe in himself. He should not believe his mind even a little.

Satru: I said, it is absolutely fine. A good man should care for his respect. Why should we listen to this kid?

Triddu: See, he is still showing off his intelligence. He will still disagree to kill Motu.

Satru: Friend, don't listen to it. It will lead you down the wrong road, which you will regret for the rest of your life.

Triddu: Now, I am strong. Its tricks won't work.

Satru: Now, be brave. Come, be ready.

Triddu: You, ready the sword. I will load the gun.

Satru: I said it is time for the *wazir* to come.

Triddu: I am fully ready.

Satru: You stand hidden in this street. I am going towards that yard.

Triddu: My gun is loaded.

[They both hide. The *wazir* comes. A soldier and a Munshi also come along.]

Mota: *Munshiji*, until tomorrow all the papers should be ready.

Munshi: As you order, Lord.

Mota: I will sign tomorrow morning.

Munshi: Okay, Lord.

[Gun shots are heard. The *wazir* cut off. Munshi and the soldier run away. Sitting in silence, they both cut the *wazir's* head with a sword]

[CURTAINS]

Scene - 7

Forest of Goddess Trikuta

[Dido is seen singing his own tune.]

Dido: Homeland has a love called life. Our homeland is our action.

Die for the homeland, it's just our religion. Drum everywhere, fearless of our homeland.

Come, take our freedom; the market is warm. Wash the dirt of subordination with pure blood.

Release the doubt of servitude from our hearts. I don't want that paradise which comes from subordination.

Be independent even if you go through hell, which looks beautiful.

[After the song]

So much time has passed, still no news has come from Jammu! Don't know where our partners have slept! They cannot do that much to send the message through the traveller. Do not know which work they are busy with. Even Bhupdev didn't come. Today, I was waiting anxiously for him.

[Seeing Bhupdev coming] Come, Bhupdev, what's the news?

Bhupdev: Brother Mota flew like a balloon in a typhoon.

Dido: Good, how?

Bhupdev: Killed yesterday evening as he entered the street. A bullet hit his chest. When he fell unconscious, we cut him into pieces with the sword.

Dido: Okay! Mota has been killed. Tell me the news about the city!

Bhupdev: The city is silent. There is a good impact on the court.

Nobody is saying anything.

Dido: What about *the Wazirani*?

Bhupdev: *Wazirani* will be *sati*.

Dido: Wow! This is great news. I am overjoyed. This is our first step towards breaking the Sikh rule. Listen, do not let Satru and Triddu get out of our hands.

Bhupdev: No, Brother. They have gone to Lahore. Kishor Singh is there. They will be in their sight.

Dido: Okay! Gulabo, Dhyanu, and Suchetu will be killed.

[Gyanu comes running]

Gyanu: Hail, Great King!

Dido: Tell, Gyanu. What is the news?

Gyanu: Today, two Sikh soldiers were killed on the banks of Tawi.

Dido: Well done, Gyanu. Today you lightened the burden of two sacks in my mind.

Gyanu: There has been an outcry among the Punjabi people. Nobody is getting out of their house because of fear.

Dido: We will stop this all. But yes, remember, don't touch the unarmed urban man. This does not suit us, warriors.

Gyanu: True words, Great King. Now, I am leaving.

Dido: Bhupu, see that the work doesn't stop. Goddess Trikuta's forest is a great place for our meeting. By putting a monarch here, we can trouble the Sikh army.

Bhupdev: Okay, I am leaving. Tomorrow we will meet at Satwari.

[Bhupdev leaves.]

Part III

Scene - 1

[At Lahore's mansion]

[Baba Mihan Singh is seated]

Mihan Singh: Since Dogra has come to Lahore, all the other officials have lost. Without any means stick to the king all the time. When Gulab Singh goes, Dhyan Singh comes, Dhyan Singh goes, Suchet Singh comes. Do not know why the whole family clings to the king. In the court, either Kishor Singh's cleverness or Gulab Singh's bravery is talked about and they do not let anything happen. Dhyan Singh's face confused the king. Do not leave him even for a moment. This concierge has made it difficult to meet the king.

[Mulakhraj Bedi arrives.]

Mr Bedi has appeared today. Tell me, how are you?

Bedi: *Babaji*, you realise why the king is dancing only to Gulab Singh's tunes? He does what he says. They do not have faith in us even for a moment.

Mihan Singh: You are also an older courtier. Suggest a way to reduce Dogra's emphasis.

Bedi: *Babaji*, I cannot suggest anything right now.

You are sensible; you should tell.

Mihan Singh: Talk to a wise man who will finish them as soon as he gets a chance.

Bedi: Babaji, you are right. But where will you find someone who is confident and is not afraid of killing and dying for money?

Mihan Singh: Oh, wait. I remember two people from Jammu whom I had hired as servants for Kanwar Khadag Singh.

Bedi: Call them for a chat.

Minha Singh: [To servant] Chandu!

[Servant comes]

Chandu: Yes, *Babaji.*

Mihan Singh: Go to Kanwar Khadag Singh's mansion. Satru and Triddu live there. Tell them *Babaji* is calling and to come soon.

Chandu: [Goes]

[Satru and Triddu come.]

Triddu: You missed us, *Babaji*?

Satru: Tell us, *Babaji.*

Mihan Singh: You two have a new job.

Triddu: We are your slaves, *Babaji*, your work is our work.

Satru: If we do not work, then who will? We are faithful to our words.

Mihan Singh: Okay, then promise me.

Satru: Take this hand. [Gives hand.]

Mihan Singh: Get Gulab Singh and Dhyan Singh out of the court somehow.

Satru: I already know that these are very bad people.

Triddu: What is the need to keep these bad people in court? It is only the right to get rid of them.

Satru: We will make him fall into such a trap that he will never forget us.

Mihan Singh: So you understood your assignment. Take these hundred Rupees to eat and drink.

Bedi: Will serve you even more.

Triddu: We have understood the work.

Mihan Singh: Go then, get started.

Bedi: The job should be done in one or two weeks.

Satru: Let's go, Triddu.

[They walk away]

Scene - 2

[At the city outskirts]

[Gulab Singh and Dhyan Singh meet]

Gulab Singh: Dhyan Singh, you did very wrong. He abused you, and you left that toxic person alive? Why did you not shoot him? I will manage everything. You are useless, Dhyan Singh.

Dhyan Singh: Brother, what did I do? I was alone and they were two. They were deliberately harassing me, but being alone, I didn't say anything to them.

Gulab Singh: You turned out to be a coward. What could they have done to you? At the most, they would have killed you. God has given a sword in our hands so that we eliminate the evildoers and improve our moral stature. When Satru abused you, you should have instantly cut his head with a sword.

Dhyan Singh: Brother! He is Kanwar's servant. Baba Mihan Singh and Bedi Mulakhraj help him. What can we outsiders do?

Gulab Singh: Worthless, get away from my sight. Brave people do not think like that. They sacrifice their life for their honour. Just yesterday, he killed Mota. Should you not be avenging him?

Dhyan Singh: Brother, whatever has happened has happened, but I will be cautious in the future for sure.

[Satru and Triddu come]

Gulab Singh: Look, both the crooks are coming towards us. You deal with Satru, and I will deal with Triddu. [To Triddu] Why did you abuse Dhyan Singh? Tell me, what did you say to him? **[Shoots at Triddu. Triddu collapses.]**

Dhyan Singh: [To Satru]

Come on, first, you killed our uncle. Now why are you being stubborn?

**[Seeing Triddu falling, Satru runs for his life.
Dhyan Singh chases him.
Yet, Satru escapes.]**

The people: [People start running haywire.] Blood, blood! Murderer! Grab him. Take him to the police station.

[People surround and grab Gulab Singh.]

A man: Let's take him to the king. Another Such a murderer should not live in this city.

Man:

One more man: It considers a human being like insects.

All: Let us go to the king.

Gulab Singh: Hey, we are the men of the king. There is no harm in killing the miscreants. We ourselves are going to the king.

[Gulab Singh is in front and people trail him.]

Scene - 3

[Court of the king]

[The king is sitting]

[Baba Mihan Singh and Bedi Mulakhraj come]

Mihan Singh: King, there has been an outcry in the city. A man was murdered in broad daylight!

King: Who did this? And why?

Mihan Singh: King, Kanwar Khadag Singh's servant, Gulab Singh, blasted bullets at him. There is an outcry among the people.

King: Call Gulab Singh.

Doorman: [On arriving.] Great King, Gulab Singh is standing at the main gate and is seeking permission to enter.

King: Take away his weapons and send him in.

Doorman: King, he is not leaving his weapon. He is saying he is a soldier of the king and would appear before him in this way alone.

King: Tell him that he is a murderer and murderers cannot bring arms in front of us.

Doorman: King, he does not agree.

King: [After removing garlands]Take this, show Gulab Singh and tell him to obey our command and leave the weapon.

[The doorman leaves and Gulab Singh walks in.]

Gulab Singh: King, victory is ours!

King: Gulab Singh, you have done the work of an idiot. You killed one of our own without any reason. Tell me, what punishment should we give you?

Gulab Singh: We have endured a lot. He is the killer of our uncle. Whenever he meets, he used to abuse us.

King: What did you gain by doing all this?

Gulab Singh: Great King, businessmen think about loss and profit. We are known to kill or to die.

King: This answer is not correct. Get out of my sight. Khushhaal Singh, he will be under your detention. Take him away.

[Gulab Singh is taken away.] [CURTAINS]

Scene - 4

A House in Village

[Roop Singh is sitting on a cot, and his wife is sitting near the hearth.]

Roop Singh: O lucky lady! Today I'm having a mild stomachache.

Pratapi: Am I a physician? Your pain has killed us.

Roop Singh: Do something.

Pratapi: I have told you to sow some carom seeds. Now enjoy the pain.

Roop Singh: It's okay! Fetch it from the shop.

Pratapi: Have I ever visited a market?

Roop Singh: Okay, warm up only a sip of water.

Pratapi: Do I not clean the dishes?

Roop Singh: Do it later, I am dying from stomach pain.

Pratapi: What about the children? They keep on yearning.

Roop Singh: Oh, lucky lady! Children will play on their own. You light the fire. Let me do the heat treatment.

Pratapi: You are sitting. Do it on your own. I am not able to light the fire all day.

[Roop Singh lights the fire and warms up the water. Sarban enters.]

Sarban: *Jai Roop Singh!*

Roop Singh: Sarban, are you okay? What is the news?

Sarban: Today, the headman Nain Singh will stay at your house.

Roop Singh: Where is he?

Sarban: I last saw him 4 miles away from here.

Roop Singh: Tell me about the battle.

Sarban: Very good.

Roop Singh: What about our men?

Sarban: Everything is fine. No one worthy died; even commoners' fatality is low.

Roop Singh: If every soldier went home, the commander would gain twice as much. Assume Nain Singh is a lucky man.

Sarban: Yes, he is very lucky.

Roop Singh: They say that Chirag Singh has won many prizes?

Sarban: Endless! He turned out to be a robust man. Age-wise, he is younger, and he also seems to be frail. But in the battlefield, he fought like a lion.

Roop Singh: Great! Chirag Singh.

Pratapi: Sarban, was Suchet also with you?

Sarban: I haven't heard this name before.

Pratapi: He was also with Nain Singh.

Roop Singh: Who are you talking about?

Son: Mummy, is talking about Uncle Suchet Singh.

Sarban: Suchet Singh? He is also with him. He is a very jolly person.

Pratapi: He has a slippery tongue. When he arrives after a holiday, he brags as if he is a warrior. I told him not to brag like that. You take as many coins as the number of men you killed in the battle. Tell me, how many people did he kill?

Roop Singh: You, keep the coins ready, he has killed so many men.

Sarban: Don't you know about him, but he has shown boldness. He has done much beyond his capabilities.

Roop Singh: You are joking. But he is also no less. He exceeds you in certain ways.

Pratapi: In fighting with a sword or in eating grains?

Remember. I made a full platter of dough and cooked it. He kept on eating. He ate the whole flour. I don't know if it is his stomach or a well.

Roop Singh: Young boys eat.

Sarban: Dear, sister! He is a handsome soldier.

Pratapi: I know that he is a soldier.

Sarban: We know that he is a good human being. He is a leader of leaders. He possesses all the characteristics of civility.

Pratapi: Do not overstate.

Roop Singh: Sarban! He is your brother. Whenever they both meet, they talk like this.

Pratapi: Your partiality towards your brother is evident. Has he ever thought about anything? Remember the last time when I caught all of his cleverness? Which new brother has he made now?

Sarban: I did not understand anything.

Roop Singh: He makes a new brother on every *Sankranti*.

Sarban: Why so?

Pratapi: His brotherhood is as circuitous as his turban.

Sarban: I think that he did not captivate the sister.

Pratapi: If he comes in front of my eyes, I can identify him in a moment. Who is his partner nowadays? Is it Kesari Singh? With whom has he teamed up now?

Sarban: Fateh Singh Maan.

Pratapi: That's not good.

Roop Singh: Sit quietly. Do not exaggerate.

Pratapi: It all seems overstated to you. His poison has more impact than snakes. I pray: Oh, God! He just spares Fateh Singh. **[Nain Singh, Suchet Singh, and companions come.]**

Nain Singh: Jaidev's brother Roop Singh, by inviting us, you troubled yourself unnecessarily. People devise ways to avoid expenses, but you are inviting expenses.

Roop Singh: Let your auspicious steps fall at our place. How can your auspicious steps be trouble for anyone? *Raghunath! Raghunath!* Nain Singh, you do not talk upright. Say it like trouble is averted and happiness abides. But when you leave, happiness goes, and worry remains.

Nain Singh: Then you intentionally keep this burden on your head.

[Pointing towards a boy] Is he your son?

Roop Singh: This is what his mother says.

Suchet Singh: So, why does he not have a face like his father's?

Pratapi: Like you said, a very good thing from your side.

But no one likes your words.

Suchet Singh: Finicky sister-in-law! Are you alive?

Pratapi: Oh, who found a brother-in-law like you? Can she die? Seeing a brother-in-law like you, respect and love will also become finicky.

Suchet Singh: Every sister-in-law considers me like a moon barring you, but why is my mind still not in them?

Pratapi: God forbid a stupid person like you will spoil others in a moment. I survived because of uninteresting behaviour.

Suchet Singh: Sister-in-law, you should train parrots, as you keep talking the whole day.

Pratapi: What will crows like you still learn?

Suchet Singh: You are talking like a parrot.

Pratapi: You just lost it.

Suchet Singh: Oh God! It will be fun if my horse runs just as fast as your tongue. My sister-in-law speaks fast, just like that.

Roop Singh: Now, it is over. Tell Nain Singh what made you come here.

Nain Singh: Roop Singh! Duggar is not in our control yet. The Great King has ordered that those who rebel bring them to Lahore. In yesterday's battle, Diwan Singh of Reasi and his companions were captured and sent to Lahore. Dido and Bhupdev have not been caught yet.

Roop Singh: Catching both is not an easy task.

Nain Singh: Listen. The people who are with them are – Fateh Singh Maan, Diwan Shankar Das, Duggal Davdi Khan, Diwan Kriparam Chopra, Sardar Atar Singh, Sardar Mohan Singh, Narayan Das Pashauriya, Ghasita Mal, and Devi Sahay.

Roop Singh: Then there is a lot of gathering. All are elected *sardars.* But there is no hope of Dido getting caught. He is very clever. He never fights pitching upfront. He knows great ways to hurt the man in front of him.

Nain Singh: Okay! We will see what happens.

[CURTAINS]

Scene - 5

[The Court of Jammu]

[Administration officer and courtier are sitting.]

Officer: So, Gulab Singh has defeated Shripat by capturing the Kot. Diwan Singh was arrested and taken to Lahore. Now, the estate of Reasi is in possession of Mian Bishanaa. The patrons of Chanas and Arliya have also come to court. Bhupdev and Dido are still roaming free. Now, they must be caught. **[Postman Chanda Singh arrives.]**

Officer: Chanda Singh, what is the news?

Chanda Singh: Oh Lord! Bhupdev drove Diwan Singh out of the jail and spread this rumour among the people that the Great King has spared his estate to us. Great moneylenders and landlords have joined hands with him. Our army is surrounded. Oh Lord, kindly send him help.

Officer: This is terrible news, Mr. Badhana! What do we do now?

Badhana: Sir, the army should be sent. Order Mian Zorawar Singh and Kishor Singh to send help from Ramgarh. Khusal's army should also be sent.

Officer: Zorawar Singh, you go to Reasi.

Zorawar Singh: Is ammunition available?

Officer: Let it be ready.

Badhana: But there is no money in the treasure.

Officer: Call Bhawani Shah.

Badhana: I am going. **[He goes.]**

Officer: If Bhawani Shah lends the money, then the work will be done.

Zorawar Singh: Why won't he lend? Will he not take interest?

[Badhana and Bhawani Shah come.]

Officer: Come, sit, Mr. Shah.

[He makes them sit near him.]

Bhawani Shah: Oh Lord! What is the order?

Officer: *Shahji*, the need has come. There is a lack of money. If you lend me one lakh Rupees, I will pay with the coming crop.

Bhawani Shah: Okay, Lord! Send the man and order the money.

Officer: Mr. Badhana writes and signs the paper to Shahji.

Badhana: Very good, Lord.

[Badhana writes and signs the paper.]

Bhawani Shah: Lord! What will you take - cash or stuff?

Officer: Cash.

Bhawani Shah: Order the cashier to bring the money with him.

Officer: Go to the cashier.

[Cashier goes]

Officer: Mian Zorawar Singh, fill gunpowder and go. Bring both Bhupdev and Diwan Singh as prisoners.

Zorawar: Okay, Lord.

Badhana: Finally, the work in Reasi is over.

Officer: Now, think about Dido as well.

Badhana: Dido should be caught smartly. Send an army contingent and a message that he has to deposit his hawk. The army will hold him captive until he gives the hawk.

Officer: Okay! Kumedan Narayan Singh, get ready.

Nain Singh: As you order, Lord!

[He leaves.]

[CURTAINS]

Scene - 6

Jungle

[Dido is seen roaming with his wife.]

Dido: Listen, lucky lady! Now our life is in danger. We don't know what will happen. Good fruits only come with good luck. But bad people are always thought to be fearful. Knowing all this, we have thought to accomplish this work. So, whatever the result, we must bear it with a smile.

Thakurian: It is true, dear husband! Otherwise, there will be no difference between a great soul like you and a common person.

Dido: May God keep all safe and sound! Don't know what will happen to us today.

[Shripat comes]

Dido: Come, *Choudhariji.*

Shripat: *Mianji*! Kindly be alert.

Dido: Why Chaudhariji?

Shripat: It is the order of the court that since Goddess Trikuta is in the state of Jammu, all the hawks are officially required here. So, it is an order for the army to take the hawk from your hands.

Dido: Wow! This is amazing. We do not accept their rule even in Jammu. And they are thrusting their occupation of Goddess Trikuta.

Shripat: Now, I will leave.

Dido: Thank you very much.

[He goes] Thakurian: What to do now?

Dido: You have to hide somewhere with this hawk.

I will deal with the rest of them.

Thakurian: Great King! As per your order.

Dido: Consider this hawk as my life.

Thakurian: Why I won't be with you in this difficult time?

Dido: Lucky lady, this hawk is my life. Consider it as my form. Once I get rid of this trouble, I will not spare anyone. Take it to another mountain.

Thakurian: [With the hawk] Don't worry about it.

[She leaves]. Narayan Singh Kumedan comes along with soldiers.]

Narayan Singh: These are the mountains of Goddess Trikuta. This is the place where Dido's hideout would be. Soldiers, search around. **[Dido is seen.]**

Look, someone is coming here. Ask him about Dido.

[The army stops; Dido comes to the front]

Commander: We want to meet Dido. Do you know where he lives?

Dido: He will be around here somewhere. Where else would he go?

Commander: Can you tell me his address?

Dido: Why not, but what's the matter? **Commander:** I just want to meet.

Dido: Come with me. **[The soldiers walk some distance.]** Here, you can camp.

Commander: We don't want to camp – we just have to go after meeting him.

Dido: Why such a hurry?

Commander: No, we will not stay.

Dido: Such a hurry? You have climbed the mountains! At least visit Goddess Trikuta. Dido will also be found.

Commander: No, no. First, I want to meet him.

Dido: What to talk to that wretch in the morning time?

Commander: I will handle all his wretchedness; you just make him meet me.

Dido: Okay.

Commander: Yes, yes!

Dido: Then tell me. I am Dido.

Commander: You have the official hawk. We are ordered to bring that hawk.

Dido: That's all? So much trouble for this? Not one, ask for ten. Goddess Trikuta has an abundance of hawks.

Commander: We are ordered to bring that hawk only. **Dido:** Okay! What objection would I have? **Commander:** Bring and present it.

Dido: Not in this way.

Commander: So, how?

Dido: Commander! You are worthy. Come to our home, have some breakfast, and then take the hawk with you.

Commander: It is not time to eat. We have food. We will eat something where we will camp.

Dido: There will be no better place than this to sit, Commander. Water is flowing nearby. Stay here. We will arrange some food and drinks.

Commander: Dido! It will not happen. We have to return soon.

Dido: We are mountainous people. Hospitality is our religion. If I send you back with an empty stomach, it will be a sin. The kitchen remains pure only when a guest eats something in our kitchen.

Commander: How can you arrange food for so many people?

Dido: You don't worry! Whatever we cook, please have it. Please take a bath in that fresh flowing water.

Commander: [To soldiers] Why, what do you say, brothers?

Soldier: As you order.

Commander: Camp here. We will spend the afternoon here.

Dido: I will get the food ready. **[Goes]**

Maahna Singh: Hospitality is a feature of the mountains.

Gahna Singh: This tradition is followed by generations.

Maahna Singh: Surain Singh, have you put chickpeas in your mouth?

Surain Singh: So what, will I sing?

Maahna Singh: Sing something, our tiredness will go away.

Surain Singh: Everyone, sit down.

Maahna Singh: Just Sing, *'Chambe the phul'*. **Surain Singh:** If you all sing, even I will.

All: Yes, yes **[All sing]**

Plumeria flower
Blossom, blossom, Plumeria flower
Leave your pleasing fragrance
Your pleasing fresh fragrance
I got a sign of love
Your beauty entranced us
Quickly grab you in arms
I want you on my mind,
I roam in the garden, near every plant
Search for you in every branch
I wandered, so I am lifeless
I become mad while bending
My hip waves undulatingly
I hold my feet carefully
I fill the box with love
I make wreaths and garlands
I wear anklets in foot
And earring in ears
I try to make up, but my friends taunt me.
My youthfulness is so drunk
My eyes are bright. Love is in my veins. Many stories in my heart.
A glimpse of a flower took away *my presence of mind*
I behave like a little girl

I say plumeria, plumeria

I keep all plumeria with myself

Someone go , bring plumeria

I don't want anything

[Dido comes in]

Dido: Commander! The food is ready. Let's have some.

[The soldiers sit down and Dido serves.]

Dido: Let's eat this dry food. Nothing more can be found in this forest.

Commander: You have created a paradise in the wilderness.

Dido: This dish is made up of green chickpeas and lentils.

Commander: Wow! Someone told the truth - chickpeas and back-biting are hard to digest.

Please give me a little more.

Dido: Commander, please eat until your stomach is full.

Commander: This bitter gourd is yummy.

Dido: This game of luck is a combination of words. Have this *badi* (a local dish made of lentils).

Commander: Oh! This *badi* is so spicy.

Dido: It takes self-realisation to reach heaven.

Commander: What have you brought?

Dido: Curry.

Commander: It's always a pleasure meeting you.

Dido: Okay! Now I get some more.

[He goes. Dido comes from behind after a while, takes out a sword, and attacks the soldiers.]

Dido: Come, soldiers. It is time you met the hawk.

[The soldiers nervously run in all directions but can't escape from Dido's hands and get killed. Corpses lay everywhere. One or two run toward the villages to save their lives.]

[CURTAINS]

Scene - 7

The Court of Jammu

[High officer and all ministers are sitting]

Officer: Today, news of great happiness has come from Lahore. Great King! Chhibbu, Baahu, and Bandraal have won the estate. At this time, Diwan Mohkam has control over Ramnagar.

Bishanaa: God's blessing is with the Great King!

Congratulations should be sent to them.

Officer: Okay, okay. But did you hear the news about Duggar?

Bishanaa: Khasal, Salaal, Kot, Chanas, and Arliya have been conquered. Shripat has also paid tribute. Dansal is captured by Mian Mota's son. Ramgarh has been taken over by Mian Kishor Singh. Zorawar Singh and Chirag Singh Agauriya are set to win the eastern estates.

Officer: Bishanaa! Your arrangement is fantastic!

What is the news about Reasi?

Bishanaa: At first, Bhupdev was surrounded in Dansaal but was successful. After that, there was news of his presence at Thanda Pani and Matehvad, but he also ran out from there to Sarod. Then, he was staying at Brahmin Sahab Roy's house.

When he was questioned, he fell at his feet and started begging and praying.

Officer: Mian Zorawar showed great bravery. A pair of gold bracelets should be sent to him as a prize.

Bishanaa: As you order, Great King!

[The postman comes running.]

Postman: Great King! Mercy! Many soldiers have been killed on the banks of Tawi.

Officer: How?

Postman: They were sitting on Tawi. They have been killed.

Officer: Who did it? And why?

Postman: It is said that Dido did this.

Officer: The army has already left to catch Dido. Any news from the mountain of Goddess Trikuta?

Bishanaa: It is possible to get the news today, but it is clear that Dido was not caught.

[Narayan Singh and Surain Singh come.]

Officer: Kumedan, have you brought the hawk?

Narayan Singh: Lord! He tricked us. All our men were killed.

See this, my arm. **[Shows him his lacerated arm.]**

I managed to safeguard my shoulder with great difficulty.

Officer: [In astonishment.] What are you saying? All men are killed? Give us a detailed report.

Narayan Singh: All men are killed except two people. First, he promised to give us the hawk, then he fed everyone, and then he attacked the oblivious people with a sword. None of our soldiers were able to get up. We have run here with great difficulty.

Officer: Oh! Deceptive wretch! Who will take responsibility for so many murders? Mian Bishanaa! What to do now?

Bishanaa: Our move did not go well. We considered him a brave warrior. But he turned out to be a fraud. When jackals and foxes damage the fields in the dark of the night, then farmers trap them to stop these activities. We should also set up a trap to catch this jackal.

Postman: Tell me which trap to set up.

Bishanaa: [After thinking] Spread this news everywhere that Dido has been given the estate of Kotli. Send him the message that the Great King is pleased by his bravery and has given him the post of minister and that he should come and take the appointment letter.

Officer: Will he agree?

Bishanaa: Yes, if someone who is carrying the message is of the Dogra community. Take the message from the court. When he comes here, be strict with him.

Officer: Lying and cheating are fair in politics. There is nothing wrong in treating him like this.

Bishanaa: Once caught, put him in jail. Then neither will he get out of the jail, nor will there be any grief.

Officer: Call Zorawar Singh.

[The servant leaves and Zorawar Singh comes.]

Zorawar: Lord! What's the order?

Officer: Did you listen to Bishanaa?

Zorawar: Yes, I did.

Officer: Then, along with your papers, you too should be ready.

Zorawar: I have another thought in my mind.

Officer: Tell me.

[Zorawar whispers something into the officer's ear.]

Officer: [Nods.] Very good.

Zorawar: I am going **[He leaves.]**

[CURTAIN]

Scene - 8

Dense Forest

[A *sadhu* comes]

Monk: [In anger] Hill men, damn you! Someone lives or dies; you do not care. You keep having fun in your own tune. Go, go away from my sight. Shake the foundation of the green hills.

[He becomes silent, closes his eyes, and begins to sing.]

"What a strange time.

All charitable, glorious, and extremely powerful people finished their breath

Cowards have held their feet firmly

How strange…

Neither shame of family,

Nor care for the country

No patriotism

Only illusion is laid

What a strange…

There is struggle in everyone's heart

The enemy is playing his trick.

Unity and brotherhood are lost.

What a strange..."

Dido: [Comes forward] Greetings, Monk.

Monk: [With angry eyes] I hate to see you, wretch! Go away from my eyes. Do not mess with me in the morning. Just like the bare peak of this mountain is shameless, so is the nature of the people here. This country will go to hell. Yes, yes! In a sea of sorrows which has no limit.

[Closes his eyes and then opens]

Dido: [To himself] *This is really a hidden sage.*

[Stands up, shivering with fear]

Monk: [Opens his eyes and looks around]

You haven't left yet?

Dido: Great King! Greetings!

Monk: [With red eyes] Why do you irritate the monk?

Go away, I did not ask you for anything.

Dido: Blessed, Great King! I pay you obeisance!

Monk: Will you leave me? Who is the king? Whose obeisance?

Dido: [With folded hands] Forgive me, Monk! I salute you.

Monk: [With angry eyes] I am not only a monk. I am a wanderer *yogi*, living in pleasure. Go and salute Ranjit Singh.

Dido: Guruji, bless us.

Monk: Who am I to do you a favour? As you sow, so shall you reap.

Dido: [Falls on the monk's feet with folded hands.] Great King, you are omniscient. Forgive me.

Monk: He embraces me unwittingly. What is your name?

Dido: My name is Dido.

Monk: Dido, Mido, and Dhido! Have you come from Takhat Hazare? You are Ranjha, go I give you Heer. **[He goes.]**

Dido: Is this a dream or reality? Heer is given, but what happiness did Ranjha get even with Heer?

[Zorawar Singh arrives.]

Dido: Come, Zorawar. How did you come to be here?

Zorawar: Brother, congratulations!

Dido: Congratulations? Why?

Zorawar: Your Majesty has given you the estate and called you to meet at Jammu.

Dido: Have you gone mad? Why will the estate be given to me?

Zorawar: No, brother. I am telling the truth. Even a proclamation has been made in the whole of Jammu.

Dido: Oh! But why?

Zorawar: Brother, the great king is happy with your bravery and has made you the minister of Jammu.

Dido: Which estate is given to me?

Zorawar: Kotli.

Dido: [Laughing] I don't believe this.

Zorawar: [Shows him a written document.] Brother, see this paper. I am not lying.

Dido: [After reading] This is okay, but how is it possible?

Zorawar: Brother, this is true! I swear.

Dido: Okay, then.

Zorawar: Then what? Take this written paper and come to court to claim the estate.

Dido: [In mind] Beggar was very popular. His words were very worthy.

[In a loud voice] Brother, I will come in one or two days.

Zorawar: Brother, if you are called by the king, you should go as soon as possible. Someone has to go in front of him even if he is not prepared and has to get the said thing done one way or the other.

Dido: I just called Jwala Singh.

Zorawar: I am with you.

Dido: [After thinking] Okay, even if there is any cheating, I have no fear. Come, let us go on an excursion in Jammu.

[CURTAINS]

Scene - 9

Court of Jammu

[Officers and Bishanaa are sitting]

Courtier: [Coming inside] Great King! A saint wants to come inside.

Officer: Who said? What is he saying?

Courtier: Great King, he wore a neat long tunic with colourful patches. He is also wearing a long hat made of lion skin with a peacock feather. In one hand, he holds a mace and a skullcap. He is strong, tall, and appears to be a heroic youth. He was coming inside, but we stopped him.

Officer: Oh! He is a saint. Call him in immediately.

[The courtier leaves and the saint comes] Officer: [Joins hands before him] Hail, *Guruji*!

Saint: [Looks around in shock.]

An inflated ego can destroy the mind. Intelligence wins everywhere. I have come to a royal temple. What is my job here?

[He leaves.]

Officer: He is a great saint. We are blessed with his arrival.

Bishanaa: Sir! Understand, now the work is done.

Officer: Make preparations for his stay.

Bishanaa: The guards are aware. Trustworthy courtiers are present. Brave wrestlers are in their own places. The army squad is ready for a salute.

Officer: Which place is arranged for the meeting?

Bishanaa: The official bungalow, which is below and decorated with paintings.

Officer: Very good. **[Dido comes with Zorawar.**

The officer and courtier stand up.]

Officer: Welcome! Welcome! **[He proceeds to shake hands as Zorawar grips him from behind.]**

Dido: What is this, Zorawar? Such a big betrayal?

Zorawar: You will teach us humanity by cheating?

Dido: Shame on your youthfulness.

Zorawar: Also, shame on this kind of hospitality.

Dido: Is this your manliness?

Zorawar: Is killing innocent guests justified?

Dido: Should a king behave deceitfully like this?

Zorawar: This is how a jackal, who destroys the farm, is treated.

Dido: Wow! I am a jackal and you a lion?

Zorawar: Yes, if you are a lion, then shake hands.

[Dido shoves Zorawar down and sprints but is surrounded by the soldiers and caught.]

Officer: Take him to the prison.

[Soldiers take Dido to the prison.]

[CURTAINS]

Scene - 10

[Jail of Jammu]

[Dido is seen as a prisoner]

Dido: [To himself.] My Duggar! I bestowed on you! Your boat is trapped in a typhoon and the high waves of Punjabi greed are trying to drown it. No matter how hearty you are, how to save you from these wretched waters? I tolerated hunger, thirst – everything and roamed in the forest. But Duggar's chain of slavery is not broken yet. This is also true that God gives success only to those who dare. *Krishnaji* says;

Doing deed is your right; Wanting result is not your work

It is okay, why expect fruit? We are not traders.

Let us be courageous and get out.

[In a loud voice] Is someone here? Is someone here?

Guard: [Comes in front.] What is the matter?

Dido: Bring water. I want to go to the toilet.

Guard: You go! I will get water.

Dido: No, I want to go near Tawi. Bring a pot full of water.

Guard: Let's go! I will go with you.

Dido: Okay! Let's go.

[Dido walks ahead holding the pot and the guard walks behind, holding his sword. Dido hits the guard's face hard and runs away. The guard shouts. People gather but Dido can't be found anywhere.]

Part IV

Scene - 1

Dido's House

Thakurian: Hello, Goddess Trikuta! It has been a long night. Even with the sunset, your mountain's beauty does not appear nice today. Even if the heat has scorched your entire body all day, the moon's splendour has made the entire environment lovely. But in all this supernatural beauty, I am going mad alone. Why has my husband taken so long to come today? My heart is terrified! I don't know what he is busy with today…

Maid: You have happily given him a break, so why are you worried?

Thakurian: Mangala, I gave him a break to make him happy; not to please myself. Why is this serpent-like worry stinging my heart? Never have I felt so sad on our separation. Now I feel like a hot tong is burning my heart.

Maid: In nervousness, the mind becomes erratic. And each doubt scares the mind by creating different shapes and forms. These doubts can't distinguish truth from lies. There is grief in separation but it is not right to allow any doubt in the mind.

Thakurian: Mangala, you are right; but the worrying has disturbed my mental peace and I can't stop crying.

Maid: Worrying is futile, Goddess; Come, let's both sing.

Thakurian: Okay, you sing a song about daytime.

Maid: Okay. [She sings.]

The sun's light is hidden. The walls also turned black.

In my *heart, there is a desire to meet my love on the lake's waves*

The rays are floating

They are gurgling and showing tantrums at the peak of mountains full of snow.

Sunshine is perfectly glowing on this

Fear of separation from lover. The glow on my face has gone.

Maid: [Seeing Dido coming] Goddess! He has come. Now, I am going to the kitchen.

[She leaves.]

Thakurian: Oh, dear husband! You spend so much time outside! I kept getting palpitations. It is so late.

Dido: Dear wife, what makes a brave lady like you anxious? You are the wife of a warrior, so why is your heart so fragile? Trust me. I am not among those who will be killed by ordinary people. We killed so many soldiers of the Sikh army today.

Thakurian: Dear, I expected this. Come, have food.

Dido: Please bring it. What have you cooked today?

Thakurian: Got a partridge, cooked it.

Dido: You did not eat anything?

Thakurian: I did not feel hungry.

Dido: It's so late!

Thakurian: Do I get hungrier than you?

Dido: I was outside.

Thakurian: I was sitting idle at home, how will I get hungry?

Dido: Dear wife! You must consider your body as a temple.

Thakurian: Seeing you, my thirst and hunger are over.

Dido: If I go out somewhere, will you fast?

Thakurian: How can I purify the kitchen, until you purify it after eating the food?

Dido: Come, let's break the fast together.

Thakurian: Mangala! Get a platter of food.

[The platter comes. Dido and Thakurian sit and eat.]

[Bhupdev comes]

Dido: Tell, Brother. What is the news?

Bhupdev: Gulab Singh's gaining the upper hand over us. People are constantly getting caught. Dharam Singh Raipuria and Chain Singh Hansali, both are caught.

Dido: This is terrible news. We lost half our strength.

Bhupdev: Dharam Singh is our arm, and Chain Singh is Duggar's braveheart.

Dido: As long as there is life in the body, the separation of our companions can't take away our religion from us.

Either worship or censure.

As alive, worldly action will go on whether Lakshmi lives or leaves

As bubbles made on the water

Either death comes now or after an era

As long as there is life in the body

Kripa Sagar on the way of justice

The *brave never get frightened.*

Bhup, now you have to work hard and make extra efforts to make up for their absence. Just tell me where are they kept captive?

Bhupdev: In Shekhupur's fort.

Dido: Okay, let them take a little rest.

[Mian Chhano arrives.]

Dido: Chhano! What is the latest news?

Chhano: A lot of brutality has occurred.

Dido: What happened, Mian Channo?

Channo: Suratu Bhageyal is cut into four pieces and is hung from the tree.

Dido: That's devastating!

Bhupdev: Brother, his death feels like my hands are chopped off.

Channo: Bhageyal bravely embraced death.

Dido: How? Tell me.

Chhano: When Gulab Singh inquired who was in favour of Bhupdev, Surat Singh came forward quickly. Again, when Gulab Singh asked them if they were helping our enemies, he said that you have just arrived, he is our king since generations. Then instantly, on the order of Gulab Singh, he was cut into four pieces and hung from the tree.

Bhupdev: Oh! Surat?

Dido: Brother, what will happen to these words?

Bhupdev: What to do now?

Dido: We cannot bring the dead back to life but can avenge them.

Bhupdev: We should avenge Bhageyal's death.

Dido: What are you thinking? Let's go and burn the market tonight.

Chhano: It is a very difficult task. Nihang Singh is guarding there.

Dido: Great. I want to kill Nihang Singh.

How are they guarding our place?

Bhupdev: The Nihang are very rude people. They do not care for anyone.

Dido: Bhupdev, what do you say?

Bhupdev: Brother, as you say!

Dido: You and Mian Channo guard in and around the market and stop to and fro movement of people. Jawahar Singh and I will deal with the guards.

Bhupdev: Brother, it is absolutely fine.

Dido: What Mian Channo, what do you say?

Channo: Good advice.

Dido: Okay, then after having food, everyone must gather at Tawi.

All: Agreed.

[CURTAINS]

Scene 2

Market of Jammu

[Nihang Singh is guarding]

Nihang Singh: My name is Gadtodan Singh and my cult is Akali. The blue dress and the guru-pleasing turban on my head are unique. I keep an arrow, *tafang, kirpan, safajung, khanda, chakra*, an iron net around the neck, and a double-barrelled gun in my hand. This is just a short-duration shift.

Even the birds cannot move their wings here. All official treasure is in my protection. The queens live in the palace, and special courts are held. No guts in any murderer to come here. I am having fun in the army, and I walk ahead of everyone. If I utter *Sat Sri Akal*, the entire village becomes empty.

Beware! Beware! Ordinary people, beware! Robbers, thieves, dacoits, everyone beware! Gadtodan Singh has come to guard. Be awake and brave.

[Dido comes to the door]

Beware! Stand there only. Who are you to come at this time?

Dido: Open the door, Singh.

Akali: First, tell me your name and work. And if you are someone ordinary, go away. Otherwise, the sword of Gadtodan Singh will cross your chest.

[Dido attacks the Akali with his sword. The Akali throws his *Khanda.* Both fight. Dido's men catch Akali. "Akali! Akal! Akal!" he says and dies.]

Dido: Break the door. **[Soldiers break the door and come inside]** Bring a cot. **[Cot is brought]** Lay it in the courtyard and fill my hookah.

[He sits on the cot and starts smoking a hookah]

My mighty soldiers! Anyone who comes close enough to kill him. Burn the office. Burn everything. Rob their treasure.

[Soldiers break the door and set a fire]

Dido: [In a loud voice] Where is the army of Punjab? Come, we are burning the market. Should I wait?

[Waits for a moment]

Come, catch us, any brave son of his mother? Come to the battlefield.

[Someone comes in front.]

[Dido drinks hookah. Men set the market ablaze. After a long time.]

Now it's morning, we have to go far. We are leaving. **[They go. The market is in a ruckus.]**

People: [crying and shouting]. Dido burnt it. Market is on fire. Help! Help!

[People walk out of their homes. The army comes. Someone brings water and tries to put off the fire.]

[CURTAINS]

Scene - 3

Lahore Court

[Maharaja and courtiers are sitting]

Doorkeeper: [Comes in.] Maharaj! Apples have come from Kashmir.

Maharaj: Who has brought them?

Doorkeeper: Maharaj, the Kashmiris have brought them.

Maharaj: Bring them here. Let's take a look.

[The doorkeeper goes and comes back with a Kashmiri lifting the rucksack on his back.]

Maharaj: Okay, open the rucksack.

[Bundles open, but dung cakes and stones are seen in place of apples.]

Maharaj: [A little embarrassed.] Cheater! What have you brought? Has Jabbar Khan joked with us? **[The Kashmiri stares.]**

Maharaj: Why don't you speak? Speak fast. Otherwise, you will be hanged.

Kashmiri: *Maharaj!* **[With folded hands]** Forgive me.

What do I speak?

Maharaj: Tell me quickly, otherwise everyone will be killed along with Jabbar Khan.

Kashmiri: Why would I bring dung cakes?

[He falls at the king's feet and cries.]

Maharaj! Forgive me.

Maharaj: Then tell. Did Jabbar Khan send apples or dung cakes?

Kashmiris: [Holding his ears.] Maharaj, he had sent apples; not dung cakes.

Maharaj: Then where are the apples?

Kashmiris: [Nodded] God knows where they are… How would I know? **[Keep hands on forehead.]** Destiny?

By God, we swear! Jabbar Khan had sent apples.

Maharaj: Okay, then where did they go? Or did you sell?

Kashmiris: [Holds his ears and cries.] Mercy!

Maharaj! I swear, I never sell official goods.

Maharaj: Then from where do these dung cakes come?

Kashmiris: Maharaj! Destiny.

[The Kashmiris look at each other.]

Maharaj: Load carrier, why are you not speaking? If you speak the truth, nothing will happen to you.

[Kashmiris cry and look around nervously.] We will find out who has taken the apples. Don't be afraid.

Kashmiris: Maharaj! I will tell you.

[Shivers and cries.]

Maharaj: Don't be afraid, tell me.

Kashmiri: Maharaj, when I was in Lahore...

[They begin to cry loudly.]

Maharaj: Hey, why are you crying? Nothing will happen to you. What happened when you were coming from Lahore?

Kashmiri: [Crying] When we stayed in Jammu at night, we found Dido.

[He cries loudly.]

Maharaj: Hey, don't cry. What did Dido say?

Kashmiri: Maharaj opened all the caskets, took out the apples, filled the rucksacks with stones and dung cakes, and beat us a lot.

[A Kashmiri puts his hand on his ribs and shows the mark.]

Maharaj: The Kashmiris should be given food and road fare. We will deal with Dido ourselves. So many *sardars* and *jagirdaars* went to catch Dido but no one could catch hold of him. Order Desa Singh to ready the army. I will go to catch Dido myself.

Gulab Singh: Maharaj! What sort of warrior is Dido? I will finish him in a moment.

Maharaj: Then why has he not been caught yet? What has

What has this big army been doing until today?

Gulab Singh: Maharaj, this is not the army's job. Those loyal like us will do this work. No need for the army. The work will be done with mind and tactics.

Maharaj: Which tactic?

Gulab Singh: You must have heard – Once there lived a rat—like Dido—in the cave of a lion. Whenever the lion rested, the rat jumped over the lion. He nibbled at the lion's hair and teased his tail. When the lion would go to catch the rat, he would run to his burrow. When the lion lay for rest, he would do it again.

Fed up, the lion raised a cat to get rid of him, from which his sufferings ended. You too raise a cat like me to accomplish this feat. Give me the responsibility and be relaxed.

Maharaj: You will take responsibility for catching Dido? **Gulab Singh:** Why not? Otherwise, what will you do with me? **Maharaj:** We want you to tie him and bring him to us.

Gulab Singh: We will do as you wish. I will not return with incomplete work.

Maharaj: Go! Ready the army. I am rewarding you this shawl.

[Gulab Singh keeps the shawl on his head]

Gulab Singh: One more request.

Maharaj: Tell me quickly.

Gulab Singh: Send the kings from these mountains who are imprisoned with me.

Maharaj: Okay. We'll leave Dharam Singh Raipuria and Chain Singh Hansali on this stipulation that they will provide you all the possible help.

[CURTAIN]

Part 5

Scene - 1

Jagti Village

[The sound of drums comes from one side]

Dam, dam, dam!

[A drummer approaches]

Drummer: Listen, villagers. This is Mian Dido's order. We have waged a war for Duggar's freedom. The heart in which blood has boiled for the love of our country; be it an old man or a young boy—Grab the sword and come to fight the war. Prepare the *langar.* Give the soldiers all the flour grains you have for banqueting the army.

[Drumming]

Dam-dam, dam-dama dam...

First man: What is he saying?

Second man: Why the proclamation?

Third man: Mian Dido's army has come. Get them refreshments.

First man: Where have they arrived?

Second man: Look, he is close.

Third man: See, great men have come.

First man: Okay, who's there?

Second man: Reasi wala Mian Chhanno, Dharm Singh Raipuriya, Jawahar Singh Aghauhariya, Sripat Dhanti Kot Wale, Chain Singh Hansali Wala, and many other warriors.

Third man: Okay, then think about which ones have to go from the village.

First man: I and Beli Brahman had decided it a very long time ago.

Second man: I will also go. Ghamma Machhi and artisan Thenu will also definitely go.

Third man: Mian Thenu keeps telling me daily. He too will definitely go.

All: Come and tell everyone the news.

[All go away. Mian Denju and artisan Thenu come.]

Mian Denju: Hey, Thenu, you also take one sword. If not made of iron, get it made of wood. Mian Dido needs soldiers. Come, you and I should get recruited.

Thenu: I'm already ready. Is there any shortage of men?

Denju: Dido wants to rebuild the kingdom. He is in dire need of artisans like you.

Thenu: Okay, the kingdom has already been completely destroyed.

Mian: Hopefully, the new kingdom will be created well.

Denju: When Dido rules, everyone will be happy. No one will have to pay taxes. Unpaid forced labour will also stop. There will be no dearth of milk, ghee, wheat, or any merchandise.

Thenu: Then it's fun. No one has been happy since this rule came. Artisans are considered as minuscule as ants.

Mian Denju: Then have fun.

Thenu: Lord Krishna has said, "Do your deeds." Should the ruler not do his deeds then? Or just say that those who don't do their deeds should not become rulers.

Mian Denju: You talked worth millions. One who is courageous can be a ruler.

Thenu: Yes! I know who is as brave as Ramu Chamar.

Mian Denju: I say that if he is made a ruler, he will skin the enemies, make shoes of them, and put them on our feet.

Thenu: What about Badhana, the butcher?

Mian Denju: We will break the enemies like a goat's neck, in a jerk. Then where will the evil be? He will fix all bad people.

Thenu: Look at Shravan, the weaver. What kind of ruler can he become?

Mian Denju: Hey, if that happens, I should be sacrificed to him since it's hard to live with your adversaries.

Thenu: Come, let's discuss. **[Goes away.]**

[Chaudhary comes]

Chaudhary: Go, bring flour, pulses, jaggery, and sugar. Whatever everyone likes to give, bring it. It is to cook for the army.

**[All women bring flour, pulses, and rice,
and put them in sacks.]**

[CURTAINS]

Scene - 2

[Dido's Camp]

[Dido and his men are sitting]

Chaudhary of *Village*: These grains have come.

Dido: Thanks *Chaudharyji*! Hand them over to the cook.

Second Choudhary: This rice sack is on my behalf.

Dido: Okay, send this to the kitchen too.

Woman: I have brought milk.

Dido: Goddess, thank you.

Another Women: Here is a pot of curd.

Dido: People of Jagati have shown a lot of love and respect. How many soldiers will *Chaudharyji* give to the army?

Chaudhary: *Mianji*, twenty soldiers are ready.

Dido: Call them. I want to meet them.

Chaudhary: This is Mian Denju, a strong young man.

He has killed a lion alone.

Dido: Wow! What a brave young man. Mian Denju, our war is with the Sikhs.

Mian Denju: Yes, I will definitely fight a war. I have wished it for a long time. When Ghamanda Singh broke the corn from our farm and went away, I was about to kill him. But my mother stopped me. Otherwise, I swear, I would have murdered him that day.

Dido: Mian Denju will become a strong soldier.

Go, work in Mian Channo's batch.

[Mian Denju goes.]

Chaudhary: This is Dara Beli. There isn't anyone who can compete with him. He comfortably lifts heavy luggage and logs.

Dido: Dara, do you want to fight the battle?

Beli: I will definitely fight the Akalis! Seeing them makes me furious.

Dido: We will be elated to have this strong, angry young man on board. Add him to Pandit Shripat's batch.

Subject: Thank you, Mianji.

[He goes away.]

Chaudhary: Here is Thenu, the artisan. He is a powerful man.

Dido: Brother, will you fight the battle?

Thenu: Yes. I would have fought the day before, but Chaudharyji stopped me. They make me work and don't pay.

Dido: You join Bhup's batch. We will force enemies to bite the dust.

Thenu: Yes, we will! **[He goes away.]**

Chaudhary: This Ghamma Machhi is also brave.

Dido: We are in need of brave people. Come on, you are with me. **[And many people come.]**

Dido: All of you join Pandit Shripat's group.

The Cook: King, the food is ready.

Dido: Serve the food to all. **[The cook serves food, and the army eats.]**

Messenger: [Comes running] Mianji, the Sikh army has arrived

Dido: Where has it arrived?

Messenger: It is close, just a mile away.

[The soldiers maintain luggage and walk]

Dido: Bhupdev, should we put up a barricade in the front? Mian Channo, what do you say?

Bhupdev: We should take the front, but it would not be a wise decision. We are fewer in number, and they are a massive army. Whatever we do, think carefully. We should further increase our strength.

[Everyone goes away. Mian Hazari is left behind.]

Hazari: Okay, no problem now. All the soldiers have gone to the army front. He is out of danger; the Sikhs cannot find him. Now what to do? Neither can I go forward, nor can I stay behind. There would definitely be a fight today but what can I do alone? What is the worst that can happen? I will be killed. I am ninety years old now. If I die, the world will not stop. Let's follow my thought, sit in the temple, and pray to Raghunathji.

[He goes away.]

[Nain Singh and Fateh Singh arrive.]

Nain Singh: *Sardarji*, this area of Basantar is rich. People here are very strong and dignified. The Earth is very fertile, and people are happy.

Fateh Singh: The financial condition of the people is also good. There is no shortage of food and water.

Nain Singh: They are no cowards; they will not hand over Dido to us.

Fateh Singh: Lay a siege around the village so that they cannot run away. **[A soldier comes running.]**

Nain Singh: Kartar Singh, what is the news?

Kartar Singh: Sir, he has run away. His father, Mian Hazari Singh, is sitting in the temple.

Fateh Singh: All our hard work has gone in vain. He has again managed to escape! Now he will cause more scuffle.

Nain Singh: Atar Singh, go get the old man.

[Atar Singh Kalal proceeds with his squad.]

Atar Singh: Get out, everyone! Temple priest, get out. What kind of meeting is this? They show connivance with the government's enemies. Go to your homes or else you will be shot. **[Hazari Singh comes out holding a sword.]**

Hazari Singh: Atar Singh, don't show your bravery. Why are you scaring the innocent people?

Atar Singh: Hey, old man, your one leg is already in the grave. Don't try to act too smart. Let go of the sword.

Hazari Singh: Atar Singh, do you want to fight with me? Go and fight with your age group.

Atar Singh: Don't talk. Leave the sword; nobody will hurt you.

Hazari Singh: If nothing happens to me, then go away from here. Why do you need to surround me?

Atar Singh: We want to take you with us.

Hazari Singh: What is my crime?

Atar Singh: Your son is an enemy of the state!

Hazari Singh: Go then, catch hold of my son.

Atar Singh: You are his father.

Hazari Singh: Then come, catch me.

Atar Singh: Won't you give up your weapon?

Hazari Singh: Am I a coward? As long as there is life in my body, I will not be in the hands of pests like you.

Atar Singh: Okay, then get ready.

Hazari Singh: Come and attack.

[Atar Singh attacks. Both fight.

Hazari Singh is killed while fighting.]

[CURTAINS]

Scene - 3

[A hill village]

[Gulab Singh's army is sitting in the camp.]

Gulab Singh: Don't know why, but wherever we go, people leave home and run away. But where Dido goes, people come to meet him with great pleasure. It has been two months since we started chasing this wretched man, but we can't get our hands on him.

Climbed the mountains, wandered in stony plains, got foot blisters from walking. Wherever we learn about his presence, we go. But by the time we reach there, he is already gone. Maybe we need to employ different tactics.

[Mian Dharm Singh comes.]

Tell everyone that wherever you go, call yourself a man of Dido.

Dharm Singh: Right, Mianji.

Gulab Singh: [Thinks] *When this Chaudhary comes, he should be captured and killed. When they do this in one or two villages, people will hand us Dido by themselves.*

[Chaudhary brings the grains.]

Gulab Singh: Who are you?

Chaudhary: Sir! I'm the Chaudhary of the village.

Gulab Singh: For whom have you brought these grains?
Chaudhary: Sir, for Dido. Heard that fighters have come.
Gulab Singh: You are Dido's friend?

Chaudhary: Sir, I have heard that he is a good man.

Gulab Singh: Do you call a thief, a robber, a dacoit, a good man?

Chaudhary: Sir! We had never heard of them in this way. He helps the poor.

Gulab Singh: How can you say such things before government officials? **[Orders]**

Teach him a lesson. **[The soldiers grab and take him away.]**

Chaudhary: Sir, what wrong have I done? I have brought grains for you too.

Gulab Singh: You have brought not for us but all for Dido.

Soldiers, tie him to the tree.

[The soldiers tie him to the tree and thrash him.]

The people: Run! Run from here. They are killing here.

Now no one will bring grain for Dido.

[A soldier comes running.]

Gulab Singh: What news have you brought?

Soldier: Sir! He is hiding on the mountain of Trikuta Devi.

Gulab Singh: How did you know?

Soldier: Sir! I myself have seen him running.

Gulab Singh: Let us move again and lay siege around the mountains of Trikuta Devi.

[Everyone leaves]

[CURTAINS]

Scene - 4

[The peak of Trikuta Devi

[Dido comes with his companions]

Dido: Friends! Today we are surrounded by enemy forces. Gulab Singh has deceived us in a big way. Also, Dharm Singh Rajpuriya, who is our childhood friend, turned out to be our enemy and a traitor. He has blocked all the ways. All the mountain Thakurs are with him. On the other side, Jagat Singh Atari Wala and Atar Singh Kalal are putting up resistance. And from the rear, Gulab Singh himself is in front with the government army of big officers. From which side can we leave now? I can't find a way by any means. Now we have no choice but to come face-to-face. There is no way out to get rid of it. Come on, friends! Get your weapons ready and trust God.

[Zorawar and Bishanaa come shouting in the background.]

Dido: These Zorawar and Bishanaa coming through the Kotli passage are eager to fight. Now, how do I use my sword on our people? No, I cannot. Come, companions! I will attack Atar Singh Kalal, the killer of my father.

[Riding a horse he charges towards Atar Singh Kalal. Atar Singh also rushes in his direction.]

Dido: [Drawing his sword.]Hey, you coward. You only know how to attack the elderly! How can you go on like this by killing my father? Now die at the hands of a young warrior!

[Dido slashes his sword on Atar Singh's head. Atar Singh falls. The army panics and retreats. Dido waits for an hour, but no one comes forward.]

Dido: Is this your bravery?

[Dido gets off his horse and sits on a rock and asks a boy:]

Oh, boy. Bring me a hookah, just want to smoke a few puffs.

The boy: [Gives a hookah.]

Dido: [After puffing] Where is Gulabu? Where is Kishor Singh's boy? If you are brave and young, then come forward [puffs again]. Come, Gulabu. Let me also see your bravery. Why are you sitting in hiding like a girl?

[Continues puffing.]

[Gulab Singh is breathless and remains quiet.]

Dido: Hey Gulabu, where are you hidden? Why are you getting these mercenaries killed? Come out in the open, show me the bravery of your sword. **[Gulab Singh remains silent. Dido challenges him again while puffing.]**

Dido: You, murderer! Sinner! You trampled the whole country in the hands of Ranjeet Singh. If you are brave, then come fight me!

[Dido keeps puffing and hurling abuses.]

Gulab Singh: Uncle Bishanaa, come here. **[Bishanaa goes.]**

[Whispers in Bishanaa's ear.] What do you see? Why don't you shoot?

[Bishanaa shoots but the bullet does not hit Dido. Gulab Singh also shoots. The bullet hits Dido's windpipe. The hookah drops from his hand and he falls on the rock.]

Dido is dead! MIAN DIDO IS DEAD! **[Was the noise, all around. The army moves forward.]**

[CURTAINS]

Scene - 5

[Garden]

[Thakurian and Mangala come]

Thakurian: Mangala, I have no idea why my heart is feeling hollow. Tell me something good that comes to your mind.

Mangala: Devi, come. Play ball with me.

Thakurian: No, Mangala. I don't feel like it. Seeing this brings back a lot of memories.

Mangala: Come, grab my hand, and play *kikli*.

Thakurian: No, my legs are not moving. Leave all this and talk about something else.

Mangala: Okay, then I will tell you a story.

Thakurian: Of sorrow or happiness?

Mangala: Both of them.

Thakurian: No, if you tell me the story of happiness that has never happened, I will think of sorrow instead of happiness. You will make me feel even less happy if you repeat the sorrowful remarks to me. Because of all the sorrow, my sorrow will double. Leave behind whatever has already occurred. Why lament over things which we never found?

Mangala: So, shall I sing a song?

Thakurian: That sounds good to me.

[The gardener and his boy come in.]

Gardener: Rise up and tie this pomegranate twig. Look at how this plant has destroyed other plants like a disobedient child that destroys their parents' reputation and compels them to hang their heads in shame. Support and tie these vines.

And do cut those random vines. They have climbed high in the garden. Our rule should be the same for everyone. You do this work, as I hoe, and pull out those useless thorny trees, weakening the other blooms in the process and using up the strength of the soil.

The boy: What is the need to do so much in this small garden? Do this here, do that there, make this bed, climb the vine upward, cut this tree? This looks like a miniature version of a large estate. You don't know that our Duggar is buried under the burden of so many trees. Even the most beautiful flowers have turned pale. Fruit trees have become useless. The worms are eating delicious fruit buds.

Gardener: Don't talk too much, what to do with all these things? You do your work. You will get the fruits of your action. Don't know before that, Gulab Singh killed Dido today.

Thakurian: What did he say? How long can I remain quiet? I am going to die with this silence. [Moves forward.] Hey, gardener! You have worms in your mouth. Where did you get the courage to speak such a thing? Was Mighty Bheem ever beaten by Duryodhan? Did Ravan ever kill Ram? You are making a river flow upstream. You, straw-like man, proclaim the death of a brave warrior. Tell me where, when, and how did you hear this? Speak, worthless! Speak quickly.

Gardener: *Devi,* forgive! Forgive me! I am not happy to say this. But what I said is absolutely true. All the hill *Sardars* favoured Gulab Singh. Dido was left alone and killed by Gulab Singh's bullet. Go to the mountain of Trikuta Maa, you will know all the truth.

Thakurian: Hey, bad news; how quickly do you spread? Why was I the last to meet you? Do you want me to remember this suffering all my life? Was I born to see to wail on the death of the bravest man of the country? Was I born to keep cursing Gulab? Go, killer gardener! I curse you for bringing this bad news! All the trees that you plant will get burnt, and your whole garden will be destroyed!

[She curses madly.]

Gardener: Greetings, holy and *sati* woman, may the supreme God fulfil your curse and reduce your suffering. Where your tears have fallen, I will plant thorny plants. I will plant an acacia tree here so that whoever comes here remembers that Queen Thakurian's tears had fallen here.

Thakurian: Mangala, our company is over now. I am going to find my husband. My soul has got wings; I have started flying. It is not my religion to live in this world now.

Mangala: Devi, do not spread thorns under your feet. Be courageous. Yours and his union was intended for this place only.

Thakurian: Mangala, our bond is forever. I will definitely find him.

[She falls to the ground and rises and sings;]

"If not there, then in paradise I will find you somewhere."

If we are together with the soul, I will see you somewhere.

Water or land, wherever I go

I will go to the moon

Or roam every star

I will search for you, my soulmate.

I will see you somewhere

He will see me somewhere.

Unconsciousness has set in; my hair is open and let loose.

I am wandering in the mountains as a saint in disguise.

He will listen to my voice somewhere

He will give me patience somewhere

Do not fade away from the heart,

Do not go away from my eyes

Have a lot of light in the heart. My hope will be fulfilled somewhere.

My thirst will be quenched somewhere

Black clouds over there will cause it to rain heavily

The statue of my lover disappeared and my heart cries at God's door.

I will have my patience somewhere. My sigh will be heard somewhere…"

[Thakurian falls to the ground, crying]

[CURTAINS]

The End

www.ingramcontent.com/pod-product-compliance
Lightning Source LLC
LaVergne TN
LVHW041058150826
845673LV00007B/1832

* 9 7 9 8 8 8 9 3 5 9 0 5 0 *